ASPECTS OF THE
FEMININE

from

The Collected Works of C. G. Jung

ASPECTS
OF THE
FEMININE

C. G. JUNG

TRANSLATED BY R.F.C. HULL

BOLLINGEN SERIES

PRINCETON UNIVERSITY PRESS

EDITORIAL NOTE

The present collection offers a range of articles and extracts from Jung's writings that convey his views on the feminine and on topics that are intrinsic or related: marriage, Eros, the mother, the maiden, and the anima/animus concept, which is a central feature of Jung's theory of personality structure. Jung did not compose a single formal statement on the psychology of women, perhaps because some of his woman colleagues—chiefly Toni Wolff, Esther Harding, and Emma Jung—were dealing separately and comprehensively with that subject.

These selections, given in chronological order, date from 1921, when Jung devoted an important section of *Psychological Types* to a discussion of the veneration of woman in poetry, to 1951, when he presented a mature discussion of the intertwined concepts of shadow, anima, and animus in a late work, *Aion*.

"Probably Jung's greatest contribution to female psychology is his concept of the animus, the contrasexual (male) archetypal component of the female psyche," Mary Ann Mattoon has recently written. "Jung tended to emphasize its negative aspects. . . . Too little has been written about the positive side of the animus. Jung mentioned its 'discriminative function,' which 'gives to woman's consciousness a capacity for reflection, deliberation, and self-knowledge,'" and its qualities of creativity, procreativity, assertiveness, and initiative. For an interpretation of approaches to the theme of the feminine by Jung and his followers, the reader is referred to Dr. Mattoon's book *Jungian Psychology in Perspective* (1981), pp. 84 ff.

W. M.

TABLE OF CONTENTS

ASPECTS OF THE FEMININE

I

THE WORSHIP OF WOMAN AND THE WORSHIP OF THE SOUL

THE LOVE PROBLEM OF A STUDENT

MARRIAGE AS A PSYCHOLOGICAL RELATIONSHIP

WOMAN IN EUROPE

ANIMA AND ANIMUS

THE WORSHIP OF WOMAN AND THE
WORSHIP OF THE SOUL*

375   The Christian principle which unites the opposites is the *worship of God*, in Buddhism it is the *worship of the self* (self-development), while in Spitteler and Goethe it is the *worship of the soul* symbolized by the *worship of woman*. Implicit in this categorization is the modern individualistic principle on the one hand, and on the other a primitive poly-daemonism which assigns to every race, every tribe, every family, every individual its specific religious principle.

376   The medieval background of *Faust* has a quite special significance because there actually was a medieval element that presided over the birth of modern individualism. It began, it seems to me, with the worship of woman, which strengthened the man's soul very considerably as a psychological factor, since the worship of woman meant worship of the soul. This is nowhere more beautifully and perfectly expressed than in Dante's *Divine Comedy*.

377   Dante is the spiritual knight of his lady; for her sake he embarks on the adventure of the lower and upper worlds. In this heroic endeavour her image is exalted into the heavenly, mystical figure of the Mother of God—a figure that has detached itself from the object and become the personification of a purely psychological factor, or rather, of those unconscious contents whose personification I have termed the *anima*. Canto XXXIII of the *Paradiso* expresses this culminating point of Dante's psychic development in the prayer of St. Bernard:

*[Section 4 of "The Type Problem in Poetry: Carl Spitteler: Prometheus and Epimetheus"]

5

> O Virgin Mother, daughter of thy Son,
> Humbler and more exalted than all others,
> Predestined object of the eternal will!
> Thou gavest such nobility to man
> That He who made mankind did not disdain
> To make Himself a creature of His making.

Verses 22–27, 29–33, 37–39 also allude to this development:

> This man, who from the nethermost abyss
> Of all the universe, as far as here,
> Has seen the spiritual existences,
> Now asks thy grace, so thou wilt grant him strength
> That he may with his eyes uplift himself
> Still higher toward the ultimate salvation.
>
> . . .
>
> I . . . proffer to thee
> All my prayers—and pray they may suffice—
> That thou wilt scatter from him every cloud
> Of his mortality, with thine own prayers,
> So that the bliss supreme may be revealed.
>
> . . .
>
> May thy protection quell his human passions!
> Lo, Beatrice and many a blessed soul
> Entreat thee, with clasped hands, to grant my wish![124]

378   The very fact that Dante speaks here through the mouth of St. Bernard is an indication of the transformation and exaltation of his own being. The same transformation also happens to Faust, who ascends from Gretchen to Helen and from Helen to the Mother of God; his nature is altered by repeated figurative deaths (Boy Charioteer, homunculus, Euphorion), until finally he attains the highest goal as Doctor Marianus. In that form Faust utters his prayer to the Virgin Mother:

> Pavilioned in the heaven's blue,
> Queen on high of all the world,
> For the holy sight I sue,
> Of the mystery unfurled.
> Sanction what in man may move
> Feelings tender and austere,
> And with glow of sacred love
> Lifts him to thy presence near.

[124] *The Divine Comedy* (trans. L. G. White), p. 187.

Souls unconquerable rise
If, sublime, thou will it;
Sinks that storm in peaceful wise
If thy pity still it.
Virgin, pure in heavenly sheen,
Mother, throned supernal,
Highest birth, our chosen Queen,
Godhead's peer eternal.

. . .

O contrite hearts, seek with your eyes
The visage of salvation;
Blissful in that gaze, arise,
Through glad regeneration.
Now may every pulse of good
Seek to serve before thy face,
Virgin, Queen of Motherhood,
Keep us, Goddess, in thy grace.[125]

379 We might also mention in this connection the symbolic attributes of the Virgin in the Litany of Loreto:

Mater amabilis	Lovable Mother
Mater admirabilis	Wonderful Mother
Mater boni consilii	Mother of good counsel
Speculum justitiae	Mirror of justice
Sedes sapientiae	Seat of wisdom
Causa nostrae laetitiae	Cause of our gladness
Vas spirituale	Vessel of the spirit
Vas honorabile	Vessel of honour
Vas insigne devotionis	Noble vessel of devotion
Rosa mystica	Mystical rose
Turris Davidica	Tower of David
Turris eburnea	Tower of ivory
Domus aurea	House of gold
Foederis arca	Ark of the covenant
Janua coeli	Gate of heaven
Stella matutina	Morning star[126]

380 These attributes reveal the functional significance of the Virgin Mother image: they show how the soul-image (anima) affects the conscious attitude. She appears as a vessel of devotion, a source of wisdom and renewal.

125 *Faust, Part Two* (trans. Wayne), pp. 284f., 288.
126 [From the *Rituale Romanum*, trans. here by A. S. B. Glover.]

381   We find this characteristic transition from the worship of woman to the worship of the soul in an early Christian document, the *Shepherd* of Hermas, who flourished about A.D. 140. This book, written in Greek, consists of a number of visions and revelations describing the consolidation of the new faith. The book, long regarded as canonical, was nevertheless rejected by the Muratori Canon. It begins as follows:

> The man who reared me sold me to a certain Rhoda in Rome. After many years, I made her acquaintance again and began to love her as a sister. One day I saw her bathing in the Tiber, and gave her my hand and helped her out of the water. When I saw her beauty I thought in my heart: "How happy I would be if I had a wife of such beauty and distinction." This was my only thought, and no other, no, not one.[127]

382   This experience was the starting-point for the visionary episode that followed. Hermas had apparently served Rhoda as a slave; then, as often happened, he obtained his freedom, and met her again later, when, probably as much from gratitude as from delight, a feeling of love stirred in his heart, though so far as he was aware it had merely the character of brotherly love. Hermas was a Christian, and moreover, as the text subsequently reveals, he was at that time already the father of a family, circumstances which would readily explain the repression of the erotic element. Yet the peculiar situation, doubtless provocative of many problems, was all the more likely to bring the erotic wish to consciousness. It is, in fact, expressed quite clearly in the thought that he would have liked Rhoda for a wife, though, as Hermas is at pains to emphasize, it is confined to this simple statement since anything more explicit and more direct instantly fell under a moral ban and was repressed. It is abundantly clear from what follows that this repressed libido wrought a powerful transformation in his unconscious, for it imbued the soul-image with life and brought about a spontaneous manifestation:[128]

----

127 [This and the following extracts were translated by an unknown hand (possibly by Baynes) from the German source used by the author. For an alternative version see *The Shepherd of Hermas* (trans. Kirsopp Lake), in *The Apostolic Fathers*, vol. 2.—TRANSLATOR.] Cf. ibid., p. 7.

128 Cf. ibid., pp. 7–9.

After a certain time, as I journeyed unto Cumae, praising God's creation in its immensity, beauty, and power, I grew heavy with sleep. And a spirit caught me up, and led me away through a pathless region where a man may not go. For it was a place full of crevices and torn by water-courses. I made my passage over the river and came upon even ground, where I threw myself upon my knees, and prayed to God, confessing my sins. While I thus prayed, the heavens opened and I beheld that lady for whom I yearned, who greeted me from heaven and said: "Hail to thee, Hermas!" While my eyes dwelt upon her, I spake, saying: "Mistress, what doest thou there?" And she answered: "I was taken up, in order to charge thee with thy sins before the Lord." I said unto her: "Dost thou now accuse me?" "No," said she, "yet hearken now unto the words I shall speak unto thee. For God, who dwelleth in heaven, and hath created the existing out of the non-existing, and hath magnified it and brought it to increase for the sake of His Holy Church, is wroth with thee, because thou has sinned against me." I answered and spake unto her: "How have I sinned against thee? When and where spake I ever an evil word unto thee? Have I not looked upon thee as a goddess? Have I not ever treated thee like a sister? Wherefore, O lady, dost thou falsely charge me with such evil and unclean things?" She smiled and said unto me: "The desire of sin arose in thy heart. Or is it not indeed a sin in thine eyes for a just man to cherish a sinful desire in his heart? Verily is it a sin," said she, "and a great one. For the just man striveth after what is just."

383   Solitary wanderings are, as we know, conducive to daydreaming and reverie. Presumably Hermas, on his way to Cumae, was thinking of his mistress; while thus engaged, the repressed erotic fantasy gradually pulled his libido down into the unconscious. Sleep overcame him, as a result of this lowering of the intensity of consciousness, and he fell into a somnambulant or ecstatic state, which itself was nothing but a particularly intense fantasy that completely captivated his conscious mind. It is significant that what then came to him was not an erotic fantasy; instead he is transported as it were to another land, represented in fantasy as the crossing of a river and a journey through a pathless country. The unconscious appears to him as an upper world in which events take place and men move about exactly as in the real world. His mistress appears before him not in an erotic fantasy but in "divine" form, seem-

ing to him like a goddess in heaven. The repressed erotic impression has activated the latent primordial image of the goddess, i.e., the archetypal soul-image. The erotic impression has evidently become united in the collective unconscious with archaic residues which have preserved from time immemorial the imprint of vivid impressions of the nature of woman— woman as mother and woman as desirable maid. Such impressions have immense power, as they release forces, both in the child and in the adult man, which fully merit the attribute "divine" i.e., something irresistible and absolutely compelling. The recognition of these forces as daemonic powers can hardly be due to moral repression, but rather to a self-regulation of the psychic organism which seeks by this change of front to guard against loss of equilibrium. For if, in face of the overwhelming might of passion, which puts one human being wholly at the mercy of another, the psyche succeeds in building up a counterposition so that, at the height of passion, the boundlessly desired object is unveiled as an idol and man is forced to his knees before the divine image, then the psyche has delivered him from the curse of the object's spell. He is restored to himself again and, flung back on himself, finds himself once more between gods and men, following his own path and subject to his own laws. The awful fear that haunts the primitive, his terror of everything impressive, which he at once senses as magic, as though it were charged with magical power, protects him in a purposive way against that most dreaded of all possibilities, loss of soul, with its inevitable sequel of sickness and death.

384   Loss of soul amounts to a tearing loose of part of one's nature; it is the disappearance and emancipation of a complex, which thereupon becomes a tyrannical usurper of consciousness, oppressing the whole man. It throws him off course and drives him to actions whose blind one-sidedness inevitably leads to self-destruction. Primitives are notoriously subject to such phenomena as running amok, going berserk, possession, and the like. The recognition of the daemonic character of passion is an effective safeguard, for it at once deprives the object of its strongest spell, relegating its source to the world of demons, i.e., to the unconscious, whence the force of passion actually springs. Exorcistic rites, whose aim is to bring back

the soul and release it from enchantment, are similarly effective in causing the libido to flow back into the unconscious.

385   This mechanism obviously worked in the case of Hermas. The transformation of Rhoda into a divine mistress deprived the actual object of her provocative and destructive power and brought Hermas under the law of his own soul and its collective determinants. Thanks to his abilities and connections, Hermas no doubt had a considerable share in the spiritual movements of his age. At that very time his brother Pius occupied the episcopal see at Rome. Hermas, therefore, was probably qualified to collaborate in the great task of his time to a greater degree than he, as a former slave, may have consciously realized. No able mind could for long have withstood the contemporary task of spreading Christianity, unless of course the barriers and peculiarities of race assigned him a different function in the great process of spiritual transformation. Just as the external conditions of life force a man to perform a social function, so the collective determinants of the psyche impel him to socialize ideas and convictions. By transforming a possible social *faux pas* into the service of his soul after having been wounded by the dart of passion, Hermas was led to accomplish a social task of a spiritual nature, which for that time was surely of no small importance.

386   In order to fit him for this task, it was clearly necessary that his soul should destroy the last possibility of an erotic attachment to the object, as this would have meant dishonesty towards himself. By consciously denying any erotic wish, Hermas merely demonstrated that it would be more agreeable for him if the erotic wish did not exist, but it by no means proved that he actually had no erotic intentions and fantasies. Therefore his sovereign lady, the soul, mercilessly revealed to him the existence of his sin, thus releasing him from his secret bondage to the object. As a "vessel of devotion" she took over the passion that was on the point of being fruitlessly lavished upon her. The last vestige of this passion had to be eradicated if the contemporary task was to be accomplished, and this consisted in delivering man from sensual bondage, from the state of primitive *participation mystique*. For the man of that age this bondage had become intolerable. The spiritual function had to be differentiated in order to restore the psychic equi-

11

librium. All philosophical attempts to do this by achieving "equanimity," most of which concentrated on the Stoic doctrine, came to grief because of their rationalism. Reason can give a man equilibrium only if his reason is already an equilibrating organ. But for how many individuals and at what periods of history has it been that? As a rule, a man needs the opposite of his actual condition to force him to find his place in the middle. For the sake of mere reason he can never forgo the sensuous appeal of the immediate situation. Against the power and delight of the temporal he must set the joy of the eternal, and against the passion of the sensual the ecstasy of the spiritual. The undeniable reality of the one must be matched by the compelling power of the other.

387 Through insight into the actual existence of his erotic desire, Hermas was able to acknowledge this metaphysical reality. The sensual libido that had previously clung to the concrete object now passed to his soul-image and invested it with the reality which the object had claimed exclusively for itself. Consequently his soul could speak to good effect and successfully enforce her demands.

388 After his conversation with Rhoda, her image vanishes and the heavens close. In her stead there now appears an "old woman in shining garments," who informs Hermas that his erotic desire is a sinful and foolish defiance of a venerable spirit, but that God is angry with him not so much on that account as because he tolerates the sins of his family. In this adroit fashion the libido is drawn away entirely from the erotic desire and in a flash is directed to the social task. An especial refinement is that the soul has discarded the image of Rhoda and taken on the appearance of an old woman, thus allowing the erotic element to recede into the background. It is later revealed to Hermas that this old woman is the Church; the concrete and personal has resolved itself into an abstraction, and the idea acquires a reality it had never before possessed. The old woman then reads to him from a mysterious book attacking heathens and apostates, but whose exact meaning he is unable to grasp. Subsequently we learn that the book sets forth a mission. Thus his sovereign lady presents him with his task, which as her knight he is pledged to accomplish. Nor is the trial of virtue lacking. For, not long after, Hermas has a vision

in which the old woman reappears, promising to return about the fifth hour in order to explain the revelation. Whereupon Hermas betook himself into the country to the appointed place, where he found a couch of ivory, set with a pillow and a cover of fine linen.

As I beheld these things lying there, I was sore amazed, and a quaking fell upon me and my hair stood on end, and a dreadful fear befell me, because I was alone in that place. But when I came once more to myself, I remembered the glory of God and took new courage; I knelt down and again confessed my sins unto God, as I had done before. Then she drew near with six young men, the which also I had seen before, and stood beside me and listened while I prayed and confessed my sins unto God. And she touched me and said: "Hermas, have done with all thy prayers and the reciting of thy sins. Pray also for righteousness, whereby thou mayest bear some of it with thee to thy house." And she raised me up by the hand and led me to the couch, and said unto the young men: "Go and build!" And when the youths were gone and we were alone, she said unto me: "Sit thee here!" I said unto her: "Mistress, let the aged first be seated." She said: "Do as I said unto thee and be thou seated." But, when I made as though to seat myself upon her right hand, she motioned me with a gesture of the hand to be seated upon her left.

As I wondered thereat, and was troubled, that I might not sit upon the right side, she said unto me: "Why art thou grieved, Hermas? The seat upon the right is for those who are already well-pleasing to God and have suffered for the Name. But to thee there lacketh much before thou canst sit with them. Yet remain as heretofore in thy simplicity, and thou shalt surely sit with them, and thus shall it be for all who shall have accomplished the work which those wrought, and endured what they suffered."[129]

389   In this situation, it would have been very easy for Hermas to give way to an erotic misunderstanding. The rendezvous has about it the feeling of a trysting-place in a "beautiful and sequestered spot," as he puts it. The rich couch waiting there is a fatal reminder of Eros, so that the terror which overcame Hermas at the sight of it is quite understandable. Clearly he must fight vigorously against these erotic associations lest he fall into a mood far from holy. He does not appear to have recognized the temptation for what it was, unless perhaps it is

[129] Cf. ibid., pp. 27ff.

tacitly admitted in the description of his terror, a touch of honesty that came more easily to the man of that time than to the man of today. For in that age man was more closely in touch with his own nature than we are, and was therefore in a position to perceive his natural reactions directly and to recognize what they were. In the case of Hermas, the confession of his sins may very well have been prompted by unholy sensations. At all events, the ensuing question as to whether he shall sit on the right hand or the left leads to a moral reprimand from his mistress. For although signs coming from the left were regarded as favourable in the Roman auguries, the left side, for both the Greeks and the Romans, was on the whole inauspicious, as the double meaning of the word "sinister" shows. But the question raised here of left and right has nothing to do with popular superstitions and is clearly of Biblical origin, referring to Matthew 25:33: "And he shall set the sheep on his right hand, but the goats on the left." Because of their guileless and gentle nature, sheep are an allegory of the good, while the unruly and lascivious nature of goats makes them an image of evil. By assigning him a seat on the left, his mistress tactfully reveals to him her understanding of his psychology.

390   When Hermas has taken his seat on her left, rather sadly, as he records, his mistress shows him a visionary scene which unrolls itself before his eyes. He beholds how the youths, assisted by ten thousand other men, build a mighty tower whose stones fit together without seams. This seamless tower, of indestructible solidity, signifies the Church, so Hermas is given to understand. *His mistress is the Church, and so is the tower.* We have seen already in the Litany of Loreto that the Virgin is named "tower of David" and "tower of ivory." The same or a similar association seems to be made here. The tower undoubtedly has the meaning of something solid and secure, as in Psalm 61:4: "For thou hast been a shelter for me, and a strong tower from the enemy." Any resemblance to the tower of Babel would involve an intense inner contradiction and must be excluded, but there may nevertheless be echoes of it, since Hermas, in company with every other thoughtful mind of that epoch, must have suffered much from the depressing spectacle of the ceaseless schisms and heretical disputes of the early Church. Such an impression may even have been his

main reason for writing these confessions, an inference supported by the fact that the mysterious book that was revealed to him inveighed against heathens and apostates. The same confusion of tongues that frustrated the building of the tower of Babel almost completely dominated the Church in the early centuries, demanding desperate efforts on the part of the faithful to overcome the chaos. Since Christendom at that time was far from being one flock under one shepherd, it was only natural that Hermas should long for the "shepherd," the *poimen,* as well as for some solid and stable structure, the "tower," that would unite in one inviolable whole the elements gathered from the four winds, the mountains and seas.

91   Earth-bound desire, sensuality in all its forms, attachment to the lures of this world, and the incessant dissipation of psychic energy in the world's prodigal variety, are the main obstacle to the development of a coherent and purposive attitude. Hence the elimination of this obstacle must have been one of the most important tasks of the time. It is therefore not surprising that, in the *Shepherd* of Hermas, it is the mastering of this task that is unfolded before our eyes. We have already seen how the original erotic stimulus and the energy it released were canalized into the personification of the unconscious complex, becoming the figure of Ecclesia, the old woman, whose visionary appearance demonstrates the spontaneity of the underlying complex. We learn, moreover, that the old woman now turns into a tower, since the tower is also the Church. This transformation is unexpected, because the connection between the tower and the old woman is not immediately apparent. But the attributes of the Virgin in the Litany of Loreto will put us on the right track, for there we find, as already mentioned, the tower associated with the Virgin Mother. This attribute has its source in the Song of Songs 4:4: "Thy neck is like the tower of David builded for an armoury," and 7:4: "Thy neck is a tower of ivory." Similarly 8:10: "I am a wall, and my breasts like towers."

392   The Song of Songs, as we know, was originally a love poem, perhaps a wedding song, which was denied canonical recognition even by Jewish scholars until very late. Mystical interpretation, however, has always loved to conceive the bride as Israel and the bridegroom as Jehovah, impelled by a sound

15

instinct to turn even erotic feelings into a relationship between God and the chosen people. Christianity appropriated the Song of Songs for the same reason, interpreting the bridegroom as Christ and the bride as the Church. To the psychology of the Middle Ages this analogy had an extraordinary appeal, and it inspired the quite unabashed Christ-eroticism of the Christian mystics, some of the best examples of which are supplied by Mechtild of Magdeburg. The Litany of Loreto was conceived in this spirit. It derived certain attributes of the Virgin directly from the Song of Songs, as in the case of the tower symbol. The rose, too, was used as one of her attributes even at the time of the Greek Fathers, together with the lily, which likewise appear in the Song of Songs (2:1): "I am the rose of Sharon, and the lily of the valleys." Images much used in the medieval hymns are the "enclosed garden" and the "sealed fountain" (Song of Songs 4:12: "A garden inclosed is my sister, my spouse; a spring shut up, a fountain sealed"). The unmistakably erotic nature of these images was explicitly accepted as such by the Fathers. Thus St. Ambrose interprets the "enclosed garden" as virginity.[130] In the same way, he[131] compares Mary with the ark of bulrushes in which Moses was found:

By the ark of bulrushes is meant the Blessed Virgin. Therefore his mother prepared the ark of bulrushes wherein Moses was placed, because the wisdom of God, which is the Son of God, chose blessed Mary the virgin and formed in her womb a man to whom he might become joined in unity of person.[132]

393   St. Augustine employs the simile (frequently used by later writers) of the *thalamus*, bridal chamber, for Mary, again in an expressly anatomical sense: "He chose for himself a chaste bridal chamber, where the bridegroom was joined to the bride,"[133] and: "He issued forth from the bridal chamber, that is from the virginal womb."[134]

---

130 *De institutione virginis*, cap. 9 (Migne, *P.L.*, vol. 16, col. 321).

131 [A. S. B. Glover, who made the following translation, points out that this *Sermo* is by *pseudo*-Ambrose. See bibliography *s.v.* Ambrose.—EDITORS.]

132 *Expositio beati Ambrosii Episcopi super Apocalypsin*, Visio 111, cap. 6, p. 38.

133 [A. S. B. Glover was unable to locate this quotation.—EDITORS.]

134 *Sermo* 192 (Migne, *P.L.*, vol. 38, col. 1013).

394 The interpretation of *vas* as the womb may therefore be taken as certain when St. Ambrose says in confirmation of St. Augustine: "Not of earth but of heaven did he choose for himself this vessel, through which he should descend to sanctify the temple of shame."[135] The designation σκεῦος (vessel) is not uncommon with the Greek Fathers. Here again there is probably an allusion to the Song of Songs, for although the designation *vas* does not appear in the Vulgate text, we find instead the image of the goblet and of drinking (7:2): "Thy navel is like a round goblet, which wanteth not liquor; thy belly is like a heap of wheat set about with lilies." The meaning of the first sentence has a parallel in the *Meisterlieder der Kolmarer Handschrift*, where Mary is compared with the widow's cruse of oil (I Kings:17:9ff.): ". . . Zarephath in the land of Zidon, whither Elijah was sent to a widow who should feed him; my body is fitly compared with hers, for God sent the prophet unto me, to change for us our time of famine."[136] With regard to the second, St. Ambrose says: "In the womb of the virgin grace increased like a heap of wheat and the flowers of the lily, even as it generated the grain of wheat and the lily."[137] In Catholic sources[138] very far-fetched passages are drawn into this vessel symbolism, as for instance Song of Songs 1:1 (DV): "Let him kiss me with the kiss of his mouth: for thy *breasts* are better than wine," and even Exodus 16:33: "Take a *pot*, and put an omer full of manna therein, and lay it up before the Lord, to be kept for your generations."

395 These associations are so contrived that they argue against rather than for the Biblical origin of the vessel symbolism. In favour of an extra-Biblical source is the fact that the medieval hymns to Mary brazenly borrowed their imagery from everywhere, so that everything that was in any way precious became associated with her. The fact that the vessel symbol is very old —it stems from the third to fourth century—is no argument against its secular origin, since even the Fathers had a weakness for non-Biblical, pagan imagery; for instance Tertullian,[139]

---

135 *De institutione virginis*, cap. 5 (Migne, *P.L.*, vol. 16, col. 313).

136 Ed. Bartsch, p. 216.

137 *De institutione virginis*, cap. 14 (Migne, *P.L.*, vol. 16, col. 327).

138 E.g., Salzer, *Sinnbilder und Beiworte Mariens*.

139 *Adversus Judaeos*, XIII (Migne, *P.L.*, vol. 2, col. 635): "That virgin earth, not yet watered by the rains nor fecundated by showers."

Augustine,[140] and others compared the Virgin with the unde-filed earth and the unploughed field, not without a sidelong glance at the Kore of the mysteries.[141] Such comparisons were based on pagan models, as Cumont has shown to be the case with the ascension of Elijah in the early medieval illustrated manuscripts, which keep closely to the Mithraic prototype. In many of its rites the Church followed the pagan model, not least in making the birth of Christ coincide with the birth of the *sol invictus*, the invincible sun. St. Jerome compares the Virgin with the sun as the mother of the light.

396   These non-Biblical allegories can have their source only in pagan conceptions still current at that time. It is therefore only just, when considering the vessel symbol, to call to mind the well-known and widespread Gnostic symbolism of the vessel. A great many incised gems have been preserved from that time which bear the symbol of a pitcher with remarkable winged bands, at once recalling the uterus with the *ligamenta lata*. This vessel is called the "vase of sins,"[142] in contrast with the hymns to Mary in which she is extolled as the "vessel of virtue." King[143] contests the former interpretation as arbitrary and agrees with Köhler[144] that the cameo-image (principally Egyptian) refers to the pots on the water-wheels that drew up water from the Nile to irrigate the fields; this would also ex-plain the peculiar bands which clearly served for fastening the pot to the water-wheel. The fertilizing function of the pot was, as King notes, expressed as the "fecundation of Isis by the seed of Osiris." Often there is on the vessel a winnowing bas-ket, probably with reference to the "mystical winnowing basket of Iakchos," or λîκνον, the figurative birthplace of the grain of wheat, symbolizing fertility.[145] There used to be a Greek marriage ceremony in which a winnowing basket filled with

---

[140] *Sermones*, 189, II (Migne, *P.L.*, vol. 38, col. 1006): "Truth is arisen from the earth, because Christ is born of a virgin."

[141] Cf. Jung, "The Psychological Aspects of the Kore."

[142] Jacques Matter, *Histoire critique du gnosticisme*. [As cited by King, *The Gnostics and Their Remains*, p. 111.]

[143] King, ibid.

[144] [Possibly H.K.E. von Köhler, "Einleitung über die Gemmen mit dem Namen der Künstler."—EDITORS.]

[145] *Symbols of Transformation*, pars. 528ff.

fruit was placed on the head of the bride, an obvious fertility charm.

397   This interpretation of the vessel is supported by the ancient Egyptian view that everything originated from the primal water, Nu or Nut, who was also identified with the Nile or the ocean. Nu is written with three pots, three water signs, and the sign for heaven. A hymn to Ptah-Tenen says: "Maker of grain, which cometh forth from him in his name Nu the Aged, who maketh fertile the watery mass of heaven, and maketh to come forth the water on the mountains to give life to men and women."[146] Wallis Budge drew my attention to the fact that the uterus symbolism exists today in the southern hinterland of Egypt in the form of rain and fertility charms. Occasionally it still happens that the natives in the bush kill a woman and take out her uterus for use in magical rites.[147]

398   When one considers how strongly the Church Fathers were influenced by Gnostic ideas in spite of their resistance to these heresies,[148] it is not inconceivable that we have in the symbolism of the vessel a pagan relic that proved adaptable to Christianity, and this is all the more likely as the worship of Mary was itself a vestige of paganism which secured for the Christian Church the heritage of the Magna Mater, Isis, and other mother goddesses. The image of the *vas Sapientiae*, vessel of wisdom, likewise recalls its Gnostic prototype, Sophia.

399   Official Christianity, therefore, absorbed certain Gnostic elements that manifested themselves in the worship of woman and found a place for them in an intensified worship of Mary. I have selected the Litany of Loreto as an example of this process of assimilation from a wealth of equally interesting material. The assimilation of these elements to the Christian symbol nipped in the bud the psychic culture of the man; for his soul, previously reflected in the image of the chosen mistress, lost its individual form of expression through this absorption. Consequently, any possibility of an individual differentiation of the soul was lost when it became repressed in the collective worship. Such losses generally have unfortunate

[146] Budge, *The Gods of the Egyptians*, I, p. 511.
[147] Talbot, *In the Shadow of the Bush*, pp. 67, 74ff.
[148] [Jung, *Aion*, chs. V and XIII.—EDITORS.]

consequences, and in this case they soon made themselves felt. Since the psychic relation to woman was expressed in the collective worship of Mary, the image of woman lost a value to which human beings had a natural right. This value could find its natural expression only through individual choice, and it sank into the unconscious when the individual form of expression was replaced by a collective one. In the unconscious the image of woman received an energy charge that activated the archaic and infantile dominants. And since all unconscious contents, when activated by dissociated libido, are projected upon external objects, the devaluation of the real woman was compensated by daemonic traits. She no longer appeared as an object of love, but as a persecutor or witch. The consequence of increasing Mariolatry was the witch hunt, that indelible blot on the later Middle Ages.

400   But this was not the only consequence. The splitting off and repression of a valuable progressive tendency resulted in a quite general activation of the unconscious. This activation could find no satisfying expression in collective Christian symbols, for an adequate expression always takes an individual form. Thus the way was paved for heresies and schisms, against which the only defence available to the Christian consciousness was fanaticism. The frenzied horror of the Inquisition was the product of over-compensated doubt, which came surging up from the unconscious and finally gave rise to one of the greatest schisms of the Church—the Reformation.

401   If I have dwelt rather longer on the symbolism of the vessel than my readers might have expected, I have done so for a definite reason, because I wanted to elucidate the psychological relations between the worship of woman and the legend of the Grail, which was so essentially characteristic of the early Middle Ages. The central religious idea in this legend, of which there are numerous variants, is the holy vessel, which, it must be obvious to everyone, is a thoroughly non-Christian image, whose origin is to be sought in extra-canonical sources.[149] From the material I have cited, it seems to me a

[149] Further evidence of the pagan root of the vessel symbolism is the "magic cauldron" of Celtic mythology. Dagda, one of the benevolent gods of ancient Ireland, possesses such a cauldron, which supplies everybody with food according to his needs or merits. The Celtic god Bran likewise possesses a cauldron of renewal. It has even been suggested that the name Brons, one of the figures in the

genuine relic of Gnosticism, which either survived the extermination of heresies because of a secret tradition, or owed its revival to an unconscious reaction against the domination of official Christianity. The survival or unconscious revivification of the vessel symbol is indicative of a strengthening of the feminine principle in the masculine psychology of that time. Its symbolization in an enigmatic image must be interpreted as a spiritualization of the eroticism aroused by the worship of woman. But spiritualization always means the retention of a certain amount of libido, which would otherwise be immediately squandered in sexuality. Experience shows that when the libido is retained, one part of it flows into the spiritualized expression, while the remainder sinks into the unconscious and activates images that correspond to it, in this case the vessel symbol. The symbol lives through the restraint imposed upon certain forms of libido, and in turn serves to restrain these forms. The dissolution of the symbol means a streaming off of libido along the direct path, or at any rate an almost irresistible urge for its direct application. But the living symbol exorcises this danger. A symbol loses its magical or, if you prefer, its redeeming power as soon as its liability to dissolve is recognized. To be effective, a symbol must be by its very nature unassailable. It must be the best possible expression of the prevailing world-view, an unsurpassed container of meaning; it must also be sufficiently remote from comprehension to resist all attempts of the critical intellect to break it down; and finally, its aesthetic form must appeal so convincingly to our feelings that no argument can be raised against it on that score. For a certain time the Grail symbol clearly fulfilled these requirements, and to this fact it owed its vitality, which, as the example of Wagner shows, is still not exhausted today, even though our age and our psychology strive unceasingly for its dissolution.[150]

Grail legend, is derived from Bran. Alfred Nutt considers that Bran, lord of the cauldron, and Brons are steps in the transformation of the Celtic Peredur Saga into the quest of the Holy Grail. It would seem, therefore, that Grail motifs already existed in Celtic mythology. I am indebted to Dr. Maurice Nicoll, of London, for this information.

[150] [Pars. 399–400 = *Ges. Werke* 6, par. 447, which there follows our par. 401.—EDITORS.]

402   Let us now recapitulate this rather lengthy discussion and see what insights have been gained. We began with the vision of Hermas, in which he saw a tower being built. The old woman, who at first had declared herself to be the Church, now explains that the tower is a symbol of the Church. Her significance is thus transferred to the tower, and it is with this that the whole remaining part of the text is concerned. For Hermas it is only the tower that matters, and no longer the old woman, let alone Rhoda. The detachment of libido from the real object, its concentration on the symbol and canalization into a symbolic function, is complete. The idea of a universal and undivided Church, expressed in the symbol of a seamless and impregnable tower, has become an unshakable reality in the mind of Hermas. The detachment of libido from the object transfers it into the subject, where it activates the images lying dormant in the unconscious. These images are archaic forms of expression which become symbols, and these appear in their turn as equivalents of the devalued objects. This process is as old as mankind, for symbols may be found among the relics of prehistoric man as well as among the most primitive human types living today. Symbol-formation, therefore, must obviously be an extremely important biological function. As the symbol can come alive only through the devaluation of the object, it is evident that the purpose it serves is to deprive the object of its value. If the object had an absolute value, it would be an absolute determining factor for the subject and would abolish his freedom of action absolutely, since even a relative freedom could not coexist with absolute determination by the object. Absolute relation to the object is equivalent to a complete exteriorization of the conscious processes; it amounts to an identity of subject and object which would render all cognition impossible. In a milder form this state still exists today among primitives. The projections we so often encounter in practical analysis are only residues of this original identity of subject and object.

403   The elimination of cognition and conscious experience resulting from such a state means a considerable impairment of the capacity for adaptation, and this weights the scales heavily against man, who is already handicapped by his nat-

ural defencelessness and the helplessness of his young. But it also produces a dangerous inferiority in the realm of affect, because an identity of feeling with the object means, firstly, that any object whatsoever can affect the subject to any degree, and secondly, any affect on the part of the subject immediately includes and violates the object. An incident in the life of a bushman may illustrate what I mean. A bushman had a little son whom he loved with the tender monkey-love characteristic of primitives. Psychologically, this love is completely auto-erotic—that is to say, the subject loves himself in the object. The object serves as a sort of erotic mirror. One day the bushman came home in a rage; he had been fishing, and had caught nothing. As usual the little fellow came running to meet him, but his father seized hold of him and wrung his neck on the spot. Afterwards, of course, he mourned for the dead child with the same unthinking abandon that had brought about his death.

404 This is a good example of the object's identity with a passing affect. Obviously this kind of mentality is inimical to any protective tribal organization and to the propagation of the species, and must therefore be repressed and transformed. This is the purpose the symbol serves, and to this end it came into being. It draws libido away from the object, devalues it, and bestows the surplus libido on the subject. This surplus exerts its effect upon the unconscious, so that the subject finds himself placed between an inner and an outer determinant, whence arises the possibility of choice and relative subjective freedom.

405 Symbols always derive from archaic residues, from racial engrams (imprints), about whose age and origin one can speculate much although nothing definite can be determined. It would be quite wrong to try to derive symbols from personal sources, for instance from repressed sexuality. Such a repression can at most supply the amount of libido required to activate the archaic engram. The engram, however, corresponds to an inherited mode of functioning which owes its existence not to centuries of sexual repression but to the differentiation of instinct in general. The differentiation of instinct was and still is a biological necessity; it is not peculiar to the human

23

species but manifests itself equally in the sexual atrophy of the worker-bee.

406   I have used the vessel symbolism as an illustration of the way symbols are derived from archaic conceptions. Just as we found the primitive notion of the uterus at the root of this symbol, we may conjecture a similar derivation in the case of the tower. The tower belongs in all probability to the category of phallic symbols in which the history of symbolism abounds. The fact that the tower, presumably symbolizing erection, appears at the very moment when Hermas has to repress his erotic fantasies at the sight of the alluring couch is not surprising. We have seen that other symbolic attributes of the Virgin and the Church are unquestionably erotic in origin, as already attested by their derivation from the Song of Songs, and that they were expressly so interpreted by the Church Fathers. The tower symbol in the Litany of Loreto has the same source and may therefore have a similar underlying meaning. The attribute "ivory" is undoubtedly erotic in origin, since it is an allusion to the tint and texture of the skin (Song of Songs 5:14: "His belly is as bright ivory"). But the tower itself is also found in an unmistakably erotic context in 8:10: "I am a wall, and my breasts like towers," which obviously refers to the jutting-out breasts with their full and elastic consistency. "His legs are as pillars of marble" (5:15), "thy neck is as a tower of ivory" (7:4), "thy nose is as the tower of Lebanon" (7:4), are equally obvious allusions to something slender and projecting. These attributes originate in tactile sensations which are transferred from the organ to the object. Just as a gloomy mood seems grey, and a joyous one bright and colourful, so also the sense of touch is influenced by subjective sexual sensations (in this case the sensation of erection) whose qualities are transferred to the object. The erotic psychology of the Song of Songs uses the images aroused in the subject for the purpose of enhancing the object's value. Ecclesiastical psychology employs these same images in order to guide the libido towards a figurative object, while the psychology of Hermas exalts the unconsciously activated image into an end in itself, using it to embody ideas that were of supreme importance for the minds of that time, namely, the consolidation and organization of the newly won Christian attitude and view of the world.

THE LOVE PROBLEM OF A STUDENT [1]

197   It is, I assure you, with no light heart that I undertake the task of opening your discussion of the love problem of a student by reading a general paper on this subject. Such a discussion is an unusual one, and presents difficulties if taken in a spirit of seriousness and with a fitting sense of responsibility.

198   Love is always a problem, whatever our age may be. In childhood, the love of one's parents is a problem, and for the old man the problem is what he has made of his love. Love is a force of destiny whose power reaches from heaven to hell. We must, I think, understand love in this way if we are to do any sort of justice to the problems it involves. They are of immense scope and complexity, not confined to any particular province but covering every aspect of human life. Love may be an ethical, a social, a psychological, a philosophical, an aesthetic, a religious, a medical, a legal, or a physiological problem, to name only a few aspects of this many-sided phenomenon. This invasion of love into all the collective spheres of life is, however, only a minor difficulty in comparison with the fact that love is also an intensely individual problem. For it means that every general criterion and rule loses its validity, in exactly the same way that religious beliefs, although constantly codified in the course of history, are always, in essence, an individual experience which bows to no traditional rule.

199   The very word "love" is itself an obstacle to our discussion. What, indeed, has not been called "love"! Beginning with the highest mystery of the Christian religion, we encounter, on the

1 [A lecture to Zurich University students, probably in Dec., 1922. Originally published in English as "The Love Problem of the Student," trans. by C. F. and H. G. Baynes from the unpublished German ms., in *Contributions to Analytical Psychology* (London and New York, 1928). For the present trans. the Baynes version has been consulted.—EDITORS.]

next-lower stages, the *amor Dei* of Origen, the *amor intellec-tualis Dei* of Spinoza, Plato's love of the Idea, and the *Gottes-minne* of the mystics. Goethe's words introduce us to the human sphere of love:

> Let now the savage instincts sleep
> And all the violence they do;
> When human love stirs in the deep
> The love of God is stirring too.

200 Here we find the love of one's neighbour, in the Christian sense as well as in the Buddhist sense of compassion, and the love of mankind as expressed in social service. Next there is love of one's country, and the love for ideal institutions such as the Church. Then comes parental love, above all mother-love, then filial love. When we come to conjugal love we leave the sphere of the spiritual and enter that intermediate realm between spirit and instinct. Here the pure flame of Eros sets fire to sexuality, and the ideal forms of love—love of parents, of country, of one's neighbour, etc.—are mingled with the lust for personal power and the desire to possess and to rule. This does not mean that all contact with instinct debases love. On the contrary, its beauty and truth and strength become the more perfect the more instinct it can absorb into itself. Only if instinct predominates does the animal come to the surface. Conjugal love can be of the kind of which Goethe says at the end of *Faust*:

> Spirit by attraction draws
> Elemental matter,
> Forges bonds no man can force
> And no angel shatter.
> Double natures single grown,
> Inwardly united,
> By Eternal Love alone
> Can it be divided.

201 But it need not necessarily be such a love. It may recall Nietzsche's words: "Two animals have lighted on each other." The love of the lover is again different. Even though the sacrament of marriage be lacking, and the pledge of a life together, this love may be transfigured by the power of fate or by its own

tragic nature. But as a rule instinct predominates, with its dark glow or its flickering fires.

202   Even this has not brought us to the limits of love. By "love" we also mean the sexual act on all levels, from officially sanctioned, wedded cohabitation to the physiological need which drives a man to prostitutes and to the mere business they make or are forced to make of love.

203   We also speak of "the love of boys," meaning homosexuality, which since classical times has lost its glamour as a social and educative institution, and now ekes out a miserable, terror-stricken existence as a so-called perversion and punishable offence, at least where men are concerned. In Anglo-Saxon countries it seems on the other hand that female homosexuality means rather more than Sapphic lyricism, since it somehow acts as a stimulus to the social and political organization of women, just as male homosexuality was an important factor in the rise of the Greek *polis*.

204   Finally, the word "love" must be stretched still further to cover all sexual perversions. There is incestuous love, and a masturbatory self-love that goes by the name of narcissism. The word "love" includes every kind of morbid sexual abomination as well as every kind of greed that has ever degraded man to the level of a beast or a machine.

205   Thus we find ourselves in the awkward position of beginning a discussion about a matter or concept whose outlines are of the vaguest and whose extent is well-nigh illimitable. At least for the purposes of the present discussion, one would like to restrict the concept of love to the problem of how a young student should come to terms with sex. But this just cannot be done, because all the meanings of the word "love" which I have already mentioned enter actively into the love problem of a student.

206   We can, however, agree to discuss the question of the way in which the average so-called normal person behaves under the conditions I have described. Disregarding the fact the "normal" person does not exist, we find, nevertheless, sufficient similarities even among individuals of the most varied types to warrant a discussion of the "average" problem. As always, the practical solution of the problem depends on two factors: the

demands and capacities of the individual, and the environmental conditions.

207   It is the duty of a speaker to present a general survey of the question under discussion. Naturally this can be done only if, as a doctor, I can give an objective account of things as they are, and abstain from that stale, moralizing talk which veils the subject with a mixture of bashfulness and hypocrisy. Moreover, I am not here to tell you what ought to be done. That must be left to those who always know what is better for other people.

208   Our theme is "The Love Problem of a Student," and I assume that "love problem" means the relation of the two sexes and is not to be construed as the "sexual problem" of a student. This provides a useful limitation of our theme, for the question of sex would need considering only so far as it is a love problem, or a problem of relationship. Hence we can exclude all those sexual phenomena that have nothing to do with relationship, such as sexual perversions (with the exception of homosexuality), masturbation, and intercourse with prostitutes. We cannot exclude homosexuality because very often it is a problem of relationship; but we can exclude prostitution because usually it does not involve a relationship, though there are exceptions which prove the rule.

209   The average solution of the love problem is, as you know, marriage. But experience shows that this statistical truth does not apply to the student. The immediate reason for this is that a student is generally not in a position to set up house. A further reason is the youthful age of most students, which, partly because of their unfinished studies, and partly because of their need for freedom to move from place to place, does not yet permit the social fixation entailed by marriage. Other factors to be considered are psychological immaturity, childish clinging to home and family, relatively undeveloped capacity for love and responsibility, lack of experience of life and the world, the typical illusions of youth, and so on. A reason that should not be underestimated is the sagacious reserve of the girl students. Their first aim is to complete their studies and take up a profession. They therefore abstain from marriage, especially from marriage with a student, who so long as he remains a student is not a desirable marriage partner for the reasons already mentioned. Another, very important, reason for the infrequency of

student marriages is the question of children. As a rule when a girl marries she wants a child, whereas a man can manage well enough for a time without children. A marriage without children has no special attraction for a woman; she prefers to wait.

210   In recent years, it is true, student marriages have become more frequent. This is due partly to the psychological changes in our modern outlook, and partly to the spread of contraceptive measures. The psychological changes that have produced, among other things, the phenomenon of the student marriage are probably the result of the spiritual upheavals of the last few decades, the total significance of which we are as yet unable to grasp. All we can say is that, as a consequence of the general dissemination of scientific knowledge and a more scientific way of thinking, a change in the very conception of the love problem has come about. Scientific objectivity has effected a rapprochement between the sacrosanct idea of man as a superior being and man as a natural being, and made it possible for *Homo sapiens* to take his place as part of the natural order. The change has an emotional as well as an intellectual aspect. Such a view works directly on the feelings of the individual. He feels released from the confines of a metaphysical system and from those moral categories which characterized the medieval outlook on the world. The taboos erected on man's exclusion from nature no longer prevail, and the moral judgments which in the last analysis always have their roots in the religious metaphysic of the age have lost their force. Within the traditional moral system everyone knows perfectly why marriage is "right" and why any other form of love is to be abhorred. But outside the system, on the playground and battlefield of nature, where man feels himself to be the most gifted member of the great family of animals, he must orient himself anew. The loss of the old standards and values amounts, at first, to moral chaos. All the hitherto accepted forms are doubted, people begin to discuss things that have long sheltered behind a moral prejudice. They boldly investigate the actual facts and feel an irresistible need to take stock of experience, to know and to understand. The eyes of science are fearless and clear; they do not flinch from gazing into moral darknesses and dirty corners. The man of today can no longer rest content with a traditional judg-

29

ment; he must know why. This search leads to the creation of new standards of value.

211   One of these is an evaluation of love in terms of hygiene. Through a franker and more objective discussion of sex a knowledge of the immense dangers of venereal disease has become much more widespread. The obligation to keep oneself healthy has superseded the guilty fears of the old morality. But this process of moral sanitation has not yet progressed to the point where public conscience would allow the same civic measures to be taken for dealing with venereal diseases as with other infectious diseases. Venereal diseases are still considered "indecent," unlike smallpox and cholera, which are morally acceptable in the drawing room. No doubt these fine distinctions will raise a smile in a more enlightened age.

212   The widespread discussion of the sexual question has brought the extraordinary importance of sexuality in all its psychic ramifications to the forefront of our social consciousness. A major contribution was made during the last twenty-five years by the much-decried psychoanalytic movement. Today it is no longer possible to brush aside the tremendous psychological importance of sex with a bad joke or a display of moral indignation. People are beginning to see the sexual question in the context of the great human problems and to discuss it with the seriousness it deserves. The natural result of this is that much that was formerly held to be beyond dispute is now open to doubt. There is, for instance, a doubt as to whether the officially sanctioned form of sexuality is the only one that is morally possible, and whether all other forms are to be condemned out of hand. The arguments for and against are gradually losing their moral acerbity, practical considerations force themselves into the discussion, and finally we are beginning to discover that legitimized sex is not *eo ipso* the equivalent of moral superiority.

213   In addition to this, the marriage problem with its usually sombre background has become a theme for romantic literature. Whereas the romance of the old style concluded with a happy betrothal or a wedding, the modern novel often begins after the marriage. In these novels, which get into everybody's hands, the most intimate problems are often treated with a lack of reticence that is positively painful. Of the veritable flood of

more or less undisguised pornographic writings we need hardly speak. A popular scientific book, Forel's *The Sexual Question,* not only had an enormous sale but found a good many imitators. In scientific literature, compilations have been produced which both in scope and in the dubious nature of their contents exceed anything found in Krafft-Ebing's *Psychopathia Sexualis,* in a way that would have been inconceivable thirty or forty years ago.

214   These widespread and widely known phenomena are a sign of the times. They make it possible for young people today to grasp the full importance of the problem of sex much earlier than they could have at any time during the last two decades. There are some who maintain that this early preoccupation with sex is unhealthy, a sign of urban degeneration. I remember reading an article fifteen years ago in Ostwald's *Annalen der Naturphilosophie,* which said, quite literally: "Primitive people like the Eskimos, Swiss, etc., have no sexual problem." It scarcely needs much reflection to see why primitives have no sexual problem; beyond the concerns of the stomach they have no other problems to worry about. Problems are the prerogative of civilized man. Here in Switzerland we have no great cities and yet such problems exist. I do not think that discussion of the sexual question is unhealthy or in the least degenerate; I see it rather as a symptom of the great psychological revolution of our time and the changes it has brought about. It seems to me that the more seriously and thoroughly we discuss this question, which is of such vital importance for man's health and happiness, the better it will be for all of us.

215   It is no doubt the serious interest shown in this question that has led to the hitherto unknown phenomenon of student marriages. Such a very recent phenomenon is difficult to judge for lack of sufficient data. In former times there were early marriages in abundance, also marriages that must have seemed socially very unstable. In itself, therefore, the student marriage is perfectly permissible. The question of children, however, is another matter. If both partners are studying, children must obviously be ruled out. But a marriage that remains artificially childless is always rather problematical. Children are the cement that holds it together as nothing else could. And it is the parents' concentration on the children which in innumera-

31

ble instances keeps alive the feeling of companionship so essential for the stability of a marriage. When there are no children the interest of each partner is directed to the other, which in itself might be a good thing. In practice, unfortunately, this mutual preoccupation is not always of an amiable kind. Each blames the other for the dissatisfaction felt by both. In these circumstances it is probably better for the wife to be studying, otherwise she is left without an object; for there are many women who cannot endure marriage without children and become unendurable themselves. If she is studying, she at least has a life outside her marriage that is sufficiently satisfying. A woman who is very set on children, and for whom children are more important than a husband, should certainly think twice before embarking on a student marriage. She should also realize that the urge to maternity often appears in imperative form only later, that is, after she is married.

216   As to whether student marriages are premature, we must take note of a fact that applies to all early marriages, namely, that a girl of twenty is usually older than a man of twenty-five, as far as maturity of judgment is concerned. With many men of twenty-five the period of psychological puberty is not yet over. Puberty is a period of illusion and only partial responsibility. The psychological difference is due to the fact that a boy, up to the time of sexual maturity, is as a rule quite childish, whereas a girl develops much earlier than he does the psychological subtleties that go hand in hand with adolescence. Into this childishness sexuality often breaks with brutal force, while, despite the onset of puberty, it often goes on slumbering in a girl until the passion of love awakens it. There are a surprising number of women whose real sexuality, even though they are married, remains virginal for years; they become conscious of it only when they fall in love with another man. That is the reason why very many women have no understanding at all of masculine sexuality—they are completely unconscious of their own. With men it is different. Sexuality bursts on them like a tempest, filling them with brute desires and needs, and there is scarcely one of them who escapes the painful problem of masturbation. But a girl can masturbate for years without knowing what she is doing.

217   The onrush of sexuality in a boy brings about a powerful

change in his psychology. He now has the sexuality of a grown man with the soul of a child. Often the flood of obscene fantasies and smutty talk with schoolfellows pours like a torrent of dirty water over all his delicate and childish feelings, sometimes smothering them for ever. Unexpected moral conflicts arise, temptations of every description lie in wait for him and weave themselves into his fantasies. The psychic assimilation of the sexual complex causes him the greatest difficulties even though he may not be conscious of its existence. The onset of puberty also brings about considerable changes in his metabolism, as can be seen from the pimples and acne that so often afflict adolescents. The psyche is disturbed in a similar manner and thrown off its balance. At this age the young man is full of illusions, which are always a sign of psychic disequilibrium. They make stability and maturity of judgment impossible. His tastes, his interests, his plans alter fitfully. He can suddenly fall head over heels in love with a girl, and a fortnight later he cannot conceive how anything of the sort could have happened to him. He is so riddled with illusions that he actually needs these mistakes to make him conscious of his own taste and individual judgment. He is still experimenting with life, and *must* experiment with it in order to learn how to judge things correctly. Hence there are very few men who have not had sexual experience of some kind before they are married. During puberty it is mostly homosexual experiences, and these are much more common than is generally admitted. Heterosexual experiences come later, not always of a very beautiful kind. For the less the sexual complex is assimilated to the whole of the personality, the more autonomous and instinctive it will be. Sexuality is then purely animal and recognizes no psychological distinctions. The most inferior woman will do; it is enough if she has the typical secondary sexual characteristics. A false step of this kind does not entitle us to draw conclusions about a man's character, as the act can easily occur at a time when the sexual complex is still split off from the psyche's influence. Nevertheless, too many experiences of this nature have a bad effect on the formation of the personality, as by force of habit they fix sexuality on too low a level and make it unacceptable to moral judgment. The result is that though the man in question is outwardly a respectable citizen, inwardly he is prey to sexual fantasies of the

33

lowest kind, or else he represses them and on some festive occasion they come leaping to the surface in their primitive form, much to the astonishment of his unsuspecting wife—assuming, of course, that she notices what is going on. A frequent accompaniment is premature coldness towards the wife. Women are often frigid from the first day of marriage because their sensation function does not respond to this kind of sexuality in their husbands. The weakness of a man's judgment at the time of psychological puberty should prompt him to reflect very deeply on the premature choice of a wife.

218   Let us now turn to other forms of relationship between the sexes that are customary during the student period. There are, as you know, characteristic liaisons between students, chiefly in the great universities of other countries. These relationships are sometimes fairly stable and may even have a psychological value, as they do not consist entirely of sexuality but also, in part, of love. Occasionally the liaison is continued into marriage. The relationship stands, therefore, considerably higher than prostitution. But as a rule it is limited to those students who were careful in the choice of their parents. It is usually a question of money, for most of the girls are dependent on their lovers for financial help, though they could not be said to sell their love for money. Very often the relationship is a beautiful episode in the girl's life, otherwise poor and empty, while for the man it may be his first intimate acquaintance with a woman, and in later life a memory on which he looks back with emotion. Often, again, there is nothing valuable in these affairs, partly owing to the man's crude sensuality, thoughtlessness, and lack of feeling, and partly owing to the frivolity and fickleness of the girl.

219   Over all these relationships hangs the Damoclean sword of their transitoriness, which prevents the formation of real values. They are passing episodes, experiments of very limited validity. Their injurious effect on the personality is due to the fact that the man gets the girl too easily, so that the value of the love-object is depreciated. It is convenient for him to dispose of his sexual problem in such a simple and irresponsible way. He becomes spoilt. But even more, the fact that he is sexually satisfied robs him of a driving-force which no young man can do without. He becomes blasé and can afford to wait. Meanwhile he

can calmly review the massed femininity passing before him until the right party turns up. Then the wedding comes along and the latest date is thrown over. This procedure adds little of advantage to his character. The low level of relationship tends to keep sexuality on a correspondingly low level of development, and this can easily lead to difficulties in marriage. Or if his sexual fantasies are repressed, the result is only too likely to be a neurotic or, worse still, a moral zealot.

220   Homosexual relations between students of either sex are by no means uncommon. So far as I can judge of this phenomenon, I would say that these relationships are less common with us, and on the continent generally, than in certain other countries where boy and girl college students live in strict segregation. I am speaking here not of pathological homosexuals who are incapable of real friendship and meet with little sympathy among normal individuals, but of more or less normal youngsters who enjoy such a rapturous friendship that they also express their feelings in sexual form. With them it is not just a matter of mutual masturbation, which in all school and college life is the order of the day among the younger age groups, but of a higher and more spiritual form which deserves the name "friendship" in the classical sense of the word. When such a friendship exists between an older man and a younger its educative significance is undeniable. A slightly homosexual teacher, for example, often owes his brilliant educational gifts to his homosexual disposition. The homosexual relation between an older and a younger man can thus be of advantage to both sides and have a lasting value. An indispensable condition for the value of such a relation is the steadfastness of the friendship and their loyalty to it. But only too often this condition is lacking. The more homosexual a man is, the more prone he is to disloyalty and to the seduction of boys. Even when loyalty and true friendship prevail the results may be undesirable for the development of personality. A friendship of this kind naturally involves a special cult of feeling, of the feminine element in a man. He becomes gushing, soulful, aesthetic, over-sensitive, etc. —in a word, effeminate, and this womanish behaviour is detrimental to his character.

221   Similar advantages and disadvantages can be pointed out in friendships between women, only here the difference in age

35

and the educative factor are not so important. The main value lies in the exchange of tender feelings on the one hand and of intimate thoughts on the other. Generally they are high-spirited, intellectual, and rather masculine women who are seeking to maintain their superiority and to defend themselves against men. Their attitude to men is therefore one of disconcerting self-assurance, with a trace of defiance. Its effect on their character is to reinforce their masculine traits and to destroy their feminine charm. Often a man discovers their homosexuality only when he notices that these women leave him stone-cold.

222 Normally, the practice of homosexuality is not prejudicial to later heterosexual activity. Indeed, the two can even exist side by side. I know a very intelligent woman who spent her whole life as a homosexual and then at fifty entered into a normal relationship with a man.

223 Among the sexual relations of the student period we must mention yet another, which is quite normal even if rather peculiar. This is the attachment of a young man to an older woman, possibly married or at any rate widowed. You will perhaps remember Jean Jacques Rousseau and his connection with Mme de Warens; this is the kind of relationship I have in mind. The man is usually rather shy, unsure of himself, inwardly afraid, sometimes infantile. He naturally seeks a mother, perhaps because he has had too much or too little love in his own family. Many women like nothing better than a man who is rather helpless, especially when they are considerably older than he is; they do not love a man's strength, his virtues and his merits, but his weaknesses. They find his infantilisms charming. If he stammers a little, he is enchanting; or perhaps he has a limp, and this excites maternal compassion and a little more besides. As a rule the woman seduces him, and he willingly submits to her mothering.

224 Not always, however, does a timid youth remain half a child. It may be that this surfeit of maternal solicitude was just what was needed to bring his undeveloped masculinity to the surface. In this way the woman educates his feeling and brings it to full consciousness. He learns to understand a woman who has experience of life and the world, is sure of herself, and thus he has a rare opportunity for a glimpse behind the scenes. But he

can take advantage of it only if he quickly outgrows this relationship, for should he get stuck in it her mothering would ruin him. Maternal tenderness is the most pernicious poison for anyone who has to equip himself for the hard and pitiless struggle of life. If he cannot let go of her apron-strings he will become a spineless parasite—for most of these women have money—and sink to the level of a lap-dog or a pet cat.

225   We must now discuss those forms of relationship which offer no solution of the sexual question for the reason that they are asexual or "platonic." If there were any reliable statistics on this subject, I believe they would show that in Switzerland the majority of students prefer a platonic relationship. Naturally, this raises the question of sexual abstinence. One often hears that abstaining from sexual intercouse is injurious to health. This view is incorrect, at least for people of the student age. Abstinence is injurious to health only when a man has reached the age when he could win a woman for himself, and should do so according to his individual inclinations. The extraordinary intensification of the sexual need that is so often felt at this time has the biological aim of forcibly eliminating the man's scruples, misgivings, doubts, and hesitations. This is very necessary, because the very idea of marriage, with all its doubtful possibilities, often makes a man panicky. It is only to be expected, therefore, that nature will push him over the obstacle. Abstention from sexual intercourse may certainly have injurious effects under these conditions, but not when there is no urgent physical or psychological need for it.

226   This brings us to the very similar question concerning the injurious effects of masturbation. When for physical or psychological reasons normal intercouse is impossible, masturbation as a safety-valve has no ill effects. Young people who come to the doctor suffering from the harmful effects of masturbation are not by any means excessive masturbationists—these usually have no need of a doctor because they are not in any sense ill —rather, their masturbation has harmful effects because it shows psychic complications and is attended by pangs of conscience or by a riot of sexual fantasies. The latter are particularly common among women. Masturbation with psychic complications is harmful, but not the ordinary, uncomplicated kind. If, however, it is continued up to the age when normal intercourse

37

becomes physically, psychologically, and socially possible, and is indulged in merely in order to avoid the necessary tasks of life, then it is harmful.

227   Platonic relationships are very important during the student period. The form they most commonly take is flirting. Flirting is the expression of an experimental attitude which is altogether appropriate at this age. It is a voluntary activity which, by tacit agreement, puts neither side under an obligation. This is an advantage and at the same time a disadvantage. The experimental attitude enables both parties to get to know each other without any immediately undesirable results. Both exercise their judgment and their skill in self-expression, adaptation, and defence. An enormous variety of experiences which are uncommonly valuable in later life can be picked up from flirting. On the other hand, the absence of any obligation can easily lead to one's becoming an habitual flirt, shallow, frivolous, and heartless. The man turns into a drawing-room hero and professional heart-breaker, never dreaming what a boring figure he cuts; the girl a coquette, and a serious man instinctively feels that she is not to be taken seriously.

228   A phenomenon that is as rare as flirting is common is the conscious cultivation of a serious love. We might call this simply the ideal, without, however, identifying it with traditional romanticism. For the development of personality, there can be no doubt that the timely awakening and conscious cultivation of deeply serious and responsible feelings are of the utmost value. A relationship of this kind can be the most effective shield against the temptations that beset a young man, as well as being a powerful incentive to hard work, loyalty, and reliability. However, there is no value so great that it does not have its unfavourable side. A relationship that is too ideal easily becomes exclusive. Through his love the young man is too much cut off from the acquaintance of other women, and the girl does not learn the art of erotic conquest because she has got her man already. Woman's instinct for possession is a dangerous thing, and it may easily happen that the man will regret all the experiences he never had with women before marriage and will make up for them afterwards.

229   Hence it must not be concluded that every relationship of this kind is ideal. There are cases where the exact opposite is

true—when, for instance, a man or girl trails round with a school sweetheart for no intelligible reason, from mere force of habit. Whether from inertia, or lack of spirit, or helplessness they simply cannot get rid of each other. Perhaps the parents on both sides find the match suitable, and the affair, begun in a moment of thoughtlessness and prolonged by habit, is passively accepted as a *fait accompli*. Here the disadvantages pile up without a single advantage. For the development of personality, acquiescence and passivity are harmful because they are an obstacle to valuable experience and to the exercise of one's specific gifts and virtues. Moral qualities are won only in freedom and prove their worth only in morally dangerous situations. The thief who refrains from stealing merely because he is in prison is not a moral personality. Though the parents may gaze benignly on this touching marriage and add their children's respectability to the tale of their own virtues, it is all a sham and a delusion, lacking real strength, and sapped by moral inertia.

230   After this brief survey of the problems as we meet them in actual life, I will, in conclusion, turn to the land of heart's desire and utopian possibilities.

231   Nowadays we can hardly discuss the love problem without speaking of the utopia of free love, including trial marriage. I regard this idea as a wishful fantasy and an attempt to make light of a problem which in actual life is invariably very difficult. It is no more possible to make life easy than it is to grow a herb of immortality. The force of gravity can be overcome only by the requisite application of energy. Similarly, the solution of the love problem challenges all our resources. Anything else would be useless patchwork. Free love would be conceivable only if everyone were capable of the highest moral achievement. The idea of free love was not invented with this aim in view, but merely to make something difficult appear easy. Love requires depth and loyalty of feeling; without them it is not love but mere caprice. True love will always commit itself and engage in lasting ties; it needs freedom only to effect its choice, not for its accomplishment. Every true and deep love is a sacrifice. The lover sacrifices all other possibilities, or rather, the illusion that such possibilities exist. If this sacrifice is not made, his illusions prevent the growth of any deep and responsible

39

feeling, so that the very possibility of experiencing real love is denied him.

232   Love has more than one thing in common with religious faith. It demands unconditional trust and expects absolute surrender. Just as nobody but the believer who surrenders himself wholly to God can partake of divine grace, so love reveals its highest mysteries and its wonder only to those who are capable of unqualified devotion and loyalty of feeling. And because this is so difficult, few mortals can boast of such an achievement. But, precisely because the truest and most devoted love is also the most beautiful, let no man seek to make it easy. He is a sorry knight who shrinks from the difficulty of loving his lady. Love is like God: both give themselves only to their bravest knights.

233   I would offer the same criticism of trial marriages. The very fact that a man enters into a marriage on trial means that he is making a reservation; he wants to be sure of not burning his fingers, to risk nothing. But that is the most effective way of forestalling any real experience. You do not experience the terrors of the Polar ice by perusing a travel-book, or climb the Himalayas in a cinema.

234   Love is not cheap—let us therefore beware of cheapening it! All our bad qualities, our egotism, our cowardice, our worldly wisdom, our cupidity—all these would persuade us not to take love seriously. But love will reward us only when we do. I must even regard it as a misfortune that nowadays the sexual question is spoken of as something distinct from love. The two questions should not be separated, for when there is a sexual problem it can be solved only by love. Any other solution would be a harmful substitute. Sexuality dished out as sexuality is brutish; but sexuality as an expression of love is hallowed. Therefore, never ask what a man does, but how he does it. If he does it from love or in the spirit of love, then he serves a god; and whatever he may do is not ours to judge, for it is ennobled.

235   I trust that these remarks will have made it clear to you that I pass no sort of moral judgment on sexuality as a natural phenomenon, but prefer to make its moral evaluation dependent on the way it is expressed.

MARRIAGE AS A PSYCHOLOGICAL RELATIONSHIP [1]

324   Regarded as a psychological relationship, marriage is a highly complex structure made up of a whole series of subjective and objective factors, mostly of a very heterogeneous nature. As I wish to confine myself here to the purely psychological problems of marriage, I must disregard in the main the objective factors of a legal and social nature, although these cannot fail to have a pronounced influence on the psychological relationship between the marriage partners.

325   Whenever we speak of a "psychological relationship" we presuppose one that is *conscious,* for there is no such thing as a psychological relationship between two people who are in a state of unconsciousness. From the psychological point of view they would be wholly without relationship. From any other point of view, the physiological for example, they could be regarded as related, but one could not call their relationship psychological. It must be admitted that though such total unconsciousness as I have assumed does not occur, there is nevertheless a not inconsiderable degree of partial unconsciousness, and the psychological relationship is limited in the degree to which that unconsciousness exists.

[1] [First published as "Die Ehe als psychologische Beziehung," in *Das Ehebuch* (Celle, 1925), a volume edited by Count Hermann Keyserling; translated by Theresa Duerr in the English version, *The Book of Marriage* (New York, 1926). The original was reprinted in *Seelenprobleme der Gegenwart* (Zurich, 1931). The essay was again translated into English by H. G. and Cary F. Baynes in *Contributions to Analytical Psychology* (London and New York, 1928), and this version has been freely consulted in the present translation.—EDITORS.]

326   In the child, consciousness rises out of the depths of unconscious psychic life, at first like separate islands, which gradually unite to form a "continent," a continuous land-mass of consciousness. Progressive mental development means, in effect, extension of consciousness. With the rise of a continuous consciousness, and not before, psychological relationship becomes possible. So far as we know, consciousness is always ego-consciousness. In order to be conscious of myself, I must be able to distinguish myself from others. Relationship can only take place where this distinction exists. But although the distinction may be made in a general way, normally it is incomplete, because large areas of psychic life still remain unconscious. As no distinction can be made with regard to unconscious contents, on this terrain no relationship can be established; here there still reigns the original unconscious condition of the ego's primitive identity with others, in other words a complete absence of relationship.

327   The young person of marriageable age does, of course, possess an ego-consciousness (girls more than men, as a rule), but, since he has only recently emerged from the mists of original unconsciousness, he is certain to have wide areas which still lie in the shadow and which preclude to that extent the formation of psychological relationship. This means, in practice, that the young man (or woman) can have only an incomplete understanding of himself and others, and is therefore imperfectly informed as to his, and their, motives. As a rule the motives he acts from are largely unconscious. Subjectively, of course, he thinks himself very conscious and knowing, for we constantly overestimate the existing content of consciousness, and it is a great and surprising discovery when we find that what we had supposed to be the final peak is nothing but the first step in a very long climb. The greater the area of unconsciousness, the less is marriage a matter of free choice, as is shown subjectively in the fatal compulsion one feels so acutely when one is in love. The compulsion can exist even when one is not in love, though in less agreeable form.

328   Unconscious motivations are of a personal and of a general nature. First of all, there are the motives deriving from parental influence. The relationship of the young man to his mother, and of the girl to her father, is the determining factor in this respect.

It is the strength of the bond to the parents that unconsciously influences the choice of husband or wife, either positively or negatively. Conscious love for either parent favours the choice of a like mate, while an unconscious tie (which need not by any means express itself consciously as love) makes the choice difficult and imposes characteristic modifications. In order to understand them, one must know first of all the cause of the unconscious tie to the parents, and under what conditions it forcibly modifies, or even prevents, the conscious choice. Generally speaking, all the life which the parents could have lived, but of which they thwarted themselves for artificial motives, is passed on to the children in substitute form. That is to say, the children are driven unconsciously in a direction that is intended to compensate for everything that was left unfulfilled in the lives of their parents. Hence it is that excessively moral-minded parents have what are called "unmoral" children, or an irresponsible wastrel of a father has a son with a positively morbid amount of ambition, and so on. The worst results flow from parents who have kept themselves artificially unconscious. Take the case of a mother who deliberately keeps herself unconscious so as not to disturb the pretence of a "satisfactory" marriage. Unconsciously she will bind her son to her, more or less as a substitute for a husband. The son, if not forced directly into homosexuality, is compelled to modify his choice in a way that is contrary to his true nature. He may, for instance, marry a girl who is obviously inferior to his mother and therefore unable to compete with her; or he will fall for a woman of a tyrannical and overbearing disposition, who may perhaps succeed in tearing him away from his mother. The choice of a mate, if the instincts have not been vitiated, may remain free from these influences, but sooner or later they will make themselves felt as obstacles. A more or less instinctive choice might be considered the best from the point of view of maintaining the species, but it is not always fortunate psychologically, because there is often an uncommonly large difference between the purely instinctive personality and one that is individually differentiated. And though in such cases the race might be improved and invigorated by a purely instinctive choice, individual happiness would be bound to suffer. (The idea of "instinct" is of course nothing more than a collective term for all kinds of organic and psychic factors whose nature is for the most part unknown.)

329   If the individual is to be regarded solely as an instrument for maintaining the species, then the purely instinctive choice of a mate is by far the best. But since the foundations of such a choice are unconscious, only a kind of impersonal liaison can be built upon them, such as can be observed to perfection among primitives. If we can speak here of a "relationship" at all, it is, at best, only a pale reflection of what we mean, a very distant state of affairs with a decidedly impersonal character, wholly regulated by traditional customs and prejudices, the prototype of every conventional marriage.

330   So far as reason or calculation or the so-called loving care of the parents does not arrange the marriage, and the pristine instincts of the children are not vitiated either by false education or by the hidden influence of accumulated and neglected parental complexes, the marriage choice will normally follow the unconscious motivations of instinct. Unconsciousness results in non-differentiation, or unconscious identity. The practical consequence of this is that one person presupposes in the other a psychological structure similar to his own. Normal sex life, as a shared experience with apparently similar aims, further strengthens the feeling of unity and identity. This state is described as one of complete harmony, and is extolled as a great happiness ("one heart and one soul")—not without good reason, since the return to that original condition of unconscious oneness is like a return to childhood. Hence the childish gestures of all lovers. Even more is it a return to the mother's womb, into the teeming depths of an as yet unconscious creativity. It is, in truth, a genuine and incontestable experience of the Divine, whose transcendent force obliterates and consumes everything individual; a real communion with life and the impersonal power of fate. The individual will for self-possession is broken: the woman becomes the mother, the man the father, and thus both are robbed of their freedom and made instruments of the life urge.

331   Here the relationship remains within the bounds of the biological instinctive goal, the preservation of the species. Since this goal is of a collective nature, the psychological link between husband and wife will also be essentially collective, and cannot

44

be regarded as an individual relationship in the psychological sense. We can only speak of this when the nature of the unconscious motivations has been recognized and the original identity broken down. Seldom or never does a marriage develop into an individual relationship smoothly and without crises. There is no birth of consciousness without pain.

31a The ways that lead to conscious realization are many, but they follow definite laws. In general, the change begins with the onset of the second half of life. The middle period of life is a time of enormous psychological importance. The child begins its psychological life within very narrow limits, inside the magic circle of the mother and the family. With progressive maturation it widens its horizon and its own sphere of influence; its hopes and intentions are directed to extending the scope of personal power and possessions; desire reaches out to the world in ever-widening range; the will of the individual becomes more and more identical with the natural goals pursued by unconscious motivations. Thus man breathes his own life into things, until finally they begin to live of themselves and to multiply; and imperceptibly he is overgrown by them. Mothers are overtaken by their children, men by their own creations, and what was originally brought into being only with labour and the greatest effort can no longer be held in check. First it was passion, then it became duty, and finally an intolerable burden, a vampire that battens on the life of its creator. Middle life is the moment of greatest unfolding, when a man still gives himself to his work with his whole strength and his whole will. But in this very moment evening is born, and the second half of life begins. Passion now changes her face and is called duty; "I want" becomes the inexorable "I must," and the turnings of the pathway that once brought surprise and discovery become dulled by custom. The wine has fermented and begins to settle and clear. Conservative tendencies develop if all goes well; instead of looking forward one looks backward, most of the time involuntarily, and one begins to take stock, to see how one's life has developed up to this point. The real motivations are sought and real discoveries are made. The critical survey of himself and his fate enables a man to recognize his peculiarities. But these insights do not come to him easily; they are gained only through the severest shocks.

331b   Since the aims of the second half of life are different from those of the first, to linger too long in the youthful attitude produces a division of the will. Consciousness still presses forward, in obedience, as it were, to its own inertia, but the unconscious lags behind, because the strength and inner resolve needed for further expansion have been sapped. This disunity with oneself begets discontent, and since one is not conscious of the real state of things one generally projects the reasons for it upon one's partner. A critical atmosphere thus develops, the necessary prelude to conscious realization. Usually this state does not begin simultaneously for both partners. Even the best of marriages cannot expunge individual differences so completely that the state of mind of the partners is absolutely identical. In most cases one of them will adapt to marriage more quickly than the other. The one who is grounded on a positive relationship to the parents will find little or no difficulty in adjusting to his or her partner, while the other may be hindered by a deep-seated unconscious tie to the parents. He will therefore achieve complete adaptation only later, and, because it is won with greater difficulty, it may even prove the more durable.

331c   These differences in tempo, and in the degree of spiritual development, are the chief causes of a typical difficulty which makes its appearance at critical moments. In speaking of "the degree of spiritual development" of a personality, I do not wish to imply an especially rich or magnanimous nature. Such is not the case at all. I mean, rather, a certain complexity of mind or nature, comparable to a gem with many facets as opposed to the simple cube. There are many-sided and rather problematical natures burdened with hereditary traits that are sometimes very difficult to reconcile. Adaptation to such natures, or their adaptation to simpler personalities, is always a problem. These people, having a certain tendency to dissociation, generally have the capacity to split off irreconcilable traits of character for considerable periods, thus passing themselves off as much simpler than they are; or it may happen that their many-sidedness, their very versatility, lends them a peculiar charm. Their partners can easily lose themselves in such a labyrinthine nature, finding in it such an abundance of possible experiences that their personal interests are completely absorbed, sometimes in a not very agreeable way, since their sole occupation then consists in track-

46

ing the other through all the twists and turns of his character. There is always so much experience available that the simpler personality is surrounded, if not actually swamped, by it; he is swallowed up in his more complex partner and cannot see his way out. It is an almost regular occurrence for a woman to be wholly contained, spiritually, in her husband, and for a husband to be wholly contained, emotionally, in his wife. One could describe this as the problem of the "contained" and the "container."

32   The one who is contained feels himself to be living entirely within the confines of his marriage; his attitude to the marriage partner is undivided; outside the marriage there exist no essential obligations and no binding interests. The unpleasant side of this otherwise ideal partnership is the disquieting dependence upon a personality that can never be seen in its entirety, and is therefore not altogether credible or dependable. The great advantage lies in his own undividedness, and this is a factor not to be underrated in the psychic economy.

33   The container, on the other hand, who in accordance with his tendency to dissociation has an especial need to unify himself in undivided love for another, will be left far behind in this effort, which is naturally very difficult for him, by the simpler personality. While he is seeking in the latter all the subtleties and complexities that would complement and correspond to his own facets, he is disturbing the other's simplicity. Since in normal circumstances simplicity always has the advantage over complexity, he will very soon be obliged to abandon his efforts to arouse subtle and intricate reactions in a simpler nature. And soon enough his partner, who in accordance with her [2] simpler nature expects simple answers from him, will give him plenty to do by constellating his complexities with her everlasting insistence on simple answers. Willynilly, he must withdraw into himself before the suasions of simplicity. Any mental effort, like the conscious process itself, is so much of a strain for the ordinary man that he invariably prefers the simple, even when it does not

---

[2] [In translating this and the following passages, I have, for the sake of clarity, assumed that the container is the man and the contained the woman. This assumption is due entirely to the exigencies of English grammar, and is not implied in the German text. Needless to say, the situation could just as easily be reversed.—TRANS.]

happen to be the truth. And when it represents at least a half-truth, then it is all up with him. The simpler nature works on the more complicated like a room that is too small, that does not allow him enough space. The complicated nature, on the other hand, gives the simpler one too many rooms with too much space, so that she never knows where she really belongs. So it comes about quite naturally that the more complicated contains the simpler. The former cannot be absorbed in the latter, but encompasses it without being itself contained. Yet, since the more complicated has perhaps a greater need of being contained than the other, he feels himself outside the marriage and accordingly always plays the problematical role. The more the contained clings, the more the container feels shut out of the relationship. The contained pushes into it by her clinging, and the more she pushes, the less the container is able to respond. He therefore tends to spy out of the window, no doubt unconsciously at first; but with the onset of middle age there awakens in him a more insistent longing for that unity and undividedness which is especially necessary to him on account of his dissociated nature. At this juncture things are apt to occur that bring the conflict to a head. He becomes conscious of the fact that he is seeking completion, seeking the contentedness and undividedness that have always been lacking. For the contained this is only a confirmation of the insecurity she has always felt so painfully; she discovers that in the rooms which apparently belonged to her there dwell other, unwished-for guests. The hope of security vanishes, and this disappointment drives her in on herself, unless by desperate and violent efforts she can succeed in forcing her partner to capitulate, and in extorting a confession that his longing for unity was nothing but a childish or morbid fantasy. If these tactics do not succeed, her acceptance of failure may do her a real good, by forcing her to recognize that the security she was so desperately seeking in the other is to be found in herself. In this way she finds herself and discovers in her own simpler nature all those complexities which the container had sought for in vain.

334   If the container does not break down in face of what we are wont to call "unfaithfulness," but goes on believing in the inner justification of his longing for unity, he will have to put up with his self-division for the time being. A dissociation is not healed

48

by being split off, but by more complete disintegration. All the powers that strive for unity, all healthy desire for selfhood, will resist the disintegration, and in this way he will become conscious of the possibility of an inner integration, which before he had always sought outside himself. He will then find his reward in an undivided self.

335   This is what happens very frequently about the midday of life, and in this wise our miraculous human nature enforces the transition that leads from the first half of life to the second. It is a metamorphosis from a state in which man is only a tool of instinctive nature, to another in which he is no longer a tool, but himself: a transformation of nature into culture, of instinct into spirit.

336   One should take great care not to interrupt this necessary development by acts of moral violence, for any attempt to create a spiritual attitude by splitting off and suppressing the instincts is a falsification. Nothing is more repulsive than a furtively prurient spirituality; it is just as unsavoury as gross sensuality. But the transition takes a long time, and the great majority of people get stuck in the first stages. If only we could, like the primitives, leave the unconscious to look after this whole psychological development which marriage entails, these transformations could be worked out more completely and without too much friction. So often among so-called "primitives" one comes across spiritual personalities who immediately inspire respect, as though they were the fully matured products of an undisturbed fate. I speak here from personal experience. But where among present-day Europeans can one find people not deformed by acts of moral violence? We are still barbarous enough to believe both in asceticism and its opposite. But the wheel of history cannot be put back; we can only strive towards an attitude that will allow us to live out our fate as undisturbedly as the primitive pagan in us really wants. Only on this condition can we be sure of not perverting spirituality into sensuality, and vice versa; for both must live, each drawing life from the other.

337   The transformation I have briefly described above is the very essence of the psychological marriage relationship. Much could be said about the illusions that serve the ends of nature and bring about the transformations that are characteristic of middle life. The peculiar harmony that characterizes mar-

49

riage during the first half of life—provided the adjustment is successful—is largely based on the projection of certain archetypal images, as the critical phase makes clear.

338   Every man carries within him the eternal image of woman, not the image of this or that particular woman, but a definite feminine image. This image is fundamentally unconscious, an hereditary factor of primordial origin engraved in the living organic system of the man, an imprint or "archetype" of all the ancestral experiences of the female, a deposit, as it were, of all the impressions ever made by woman—in short, an inherited system of psychic adaptation. Even if no women existed, it would still be possible, at any given time, to deduce from this unconscious image exactly how a woman would have to be constituted psychically. The same is true of the woman: she too has her inborn image of man. Actually, we know from experience that it would be more accurate to describe it as an image of *men,* whereas in the case of the man it is rather the image of *woman.* Since this image is unconscious, it is always unconsciously projected upon the person of the beloved, and is one of the chief reasons for passionate attraction or aversion. I have called this image the "anima," and I find the scholastic question *Habet mulier animam?* especially interesting, since in my view it is an intelligent one inasmuch as the doubt seems justified. Woman has no anima, no soul, but she has an *animus.* The anima has an erotic, emotional character, the animus a rationalizing one. Hence most of what men say about feminine eroticism, and particularly about the emotional life of women, is derived from their own anima projections and distorted accordingly. On the other hand, the astonishing assumptions and fantasies that women make about men come from the activity of the animus, who produces an inexhaustible supply of illogical arguments and false explanations.

339   Anima and animus are both characterized by an extraordinary many-sidedness. In a marriage it is always the contained who projects this image upon the container, while the latter is only partially able to project his unconscious image upon his partner. The more unified and simple this partner is, the less complete the projection. In which case, this highly fascinating image hangs as it were in mid air, as though waiting to be filled out by a living person. There are certain types of women who

seem to be made by nature to attract anima projections; indeed one could almost speak of a definite "anima type." The so-called "sphinx-like" character is an indispensable part of their equipment, also an equivocalness, an intriguing elusiveness—not an indefinite blur that offers nothing, but an indefiniteness that seems full of promises, like the speaking silence of a Mona Lisa. A woman of this kind is both old and young, mother and daughter, of more than doubtful chastity, childlike, and yet endowed with a naïve cunning that is extremely disarming to men.[3] Not every man of real intellectual power can be an animus, for the animus must be a master not so much of fine ideas as of fine words—words seemingly full of meaning which purport to leave a great deal unsaid. He must also belong to the "misunderstood" class, or be in some way at odds with his environment, so that the idea of self-sacrifice can insinuate itself. He must be a rather questionable hero, a man with possibilities, which is not to say that an animus projection may not discover a real hero long before he has become perceptible to the sluggish wits of the man of "average intelligence."[4]

40   For man as well as for woman, in so far as they are "containers," the filling out of this image is an experience fraught with consequences, for it holds the possibility of finding one's own complexities answered by a corresponding diversity. Wide vistas seem to open up in which one feels oneself embraced and contained. I say "seem" advisedly, because the experience may be two-faced. Just as the animus projection of a woman can often pick on a man of real significance who is not recognized by the mass, and can actually help him to achieve his true destiny with her moral support, so a man can create for himself a *femme inspiratrice* by his anima projection. But more often it turns out to be an illusion with destructive consequences, a failure because his faith was not sufficiently strong. To the pessimists I would say that these primordial psychic images have an extraordinarily positive value, but I must warn the optimists against

3 There are excellent descriptions of this type in H. Rider Haggard's *She* (London, 1887) and Pierre Benoît's *L'Atlantide* (Paris, 1920; trans. by Mary C. Tongue and Mary Ross as *Atlantida*, New York, 1920).

4 A passably good account of the animus is to be found in Marie Hay's book *The Evil Vineyard* (New York, 1923), also in Elinor Wylie's *Jennifer Lorn* (New York, 1923) and Selma Lagerlöf's *Gösta Berlings Saga* (1891; English trans. by P. B. Flach, *The Story of Gösta Berling*, 1898).

blinding fantasies and the likelihood of the most absurd aberrations.

341   One should on no account take this projection for an individual and conscious relationship. In its first stages it is far from that, for it creates a compulsive dependence based on unconscious motives other than the biological ones. Rider Haggard's *She* gives some indication of the curious world of ideas that underlies the anima projection. They are in essence spiritual contents, often in erotic disguise, obvious fragments of a primitive mythological mentality that consists of archetypes, and whose totality constitutes the collective unconscious. Accordingly, such a relationship is at bottom collective and not individual. (Benoît, who created in *L'Atlantide* a fantasy figure similar even in details to "She," denies having plagiarized Rider Haggard.)

342   If such a projection fastens on to one of the marriage partners, a collective spiritual relationship conflicts with the collective biological one and produces in the container the division or disintegration I have described above. If he is able to hold his head above water, he will find himself through this very conflict. In that case the projection, though dangerous in itself, will have helped him to pass from a collective to an individual relationship. This amounts to full conscious realization of the relationship that marriage brings. Since the aim of this paper is a discussion of the psychology of marriage, the psychology of projection cannot concern us here. It is sufficient to mention it as a fact.

343   One can hardly deal with the psychological marriage relationship without mentioning, even at the risk of misunderstanding, the nature of its critical transitions. As is well known, one understands nothing psychological unless one has experienced it oneself. Not that this ever prevents anyone from feeling convinced that his own judgment is the only true and competent one. This disconcerting fact comes from the necessary overvaluation of the momentary content of consciousness, for without this concentration of attention one could not be conscious at all. Thus it is that every period of life has its own psychological truth, and the same applies to every stage of psychological development. There are even stages which only the few can reach, it being a question of race, family, education, talent, and passion. Nature is aristocratic. The normal man is a fiction, al-

though certain generally valid laws do exist. Psychic life is a development that can easily be arrested on the lowest levels. It is as though every individual had a specific gravity, in accordance with which he either rises, or sinks down, to the level where he reaches his limit. His views and convictions will be determined accordingly. No wonder, then, that by far the greater number of marriages reach their upper psychological limit in fulfilment of the biological aim, without injury to spiritual or moral health. Relatively few people fall into deeper disharmony with themselves. Where there is a great deal of pressure from outside, the conflict is unable to develop much dramatic tension for sheer lack of energy. Psychological insecurity, however, increases in proportion to social security, unconsciously at first, causing neuroses, then consciously, bringing with it separations, discord, divorces, and other marital disorders. On still higher levels, new possibilities of psychological development are discerned, touching on the sphere of religion where critical judgment comes to a halt.

344   Progress may be permanently arrested on any of these levels, with complete unconsciousness of what might have followed at the next stage of development. As a rule graduation to the next stage is barred by violent prejudices and superstitious fears. This, however, serves a most useful purpose, since a man who is compelled by accident to live at a level too high for him becomes a fool and a menace.

345   Nature is not only aristocratic, she is also esoteric. Yet no man of understanding will thereby be induced to make a secret of what he knows, for he realizes only too well that the secret of psychic development can never be betrayed, simply because that development is a question of individual capacity.

WOMAN IN EUROPE [1]

> You call yourself free? Your domi-
> nant thought I would hear, and
> not that you have escaped from a
> yoke. Are you one of those who
> had the right to escape from a
> yoke? There are some who threw
> away their last value when they
> threw away their servitude.
>
> *Thus Spake Zarathustra*

[36] To write about woman in Europe today is such a hazardous undertaking that I would scarcely have ventured to do so without a pressing invitation. Have we anything of fundamental importance to say about Europe? Is anyone sufficiently detached? Are we not all involved in some programme or experiment, or caught in some critical retrospect that clouds our judgment? And in regard to woman, cannot the same questions be asked? Moreover, what can a man say about woman, his own opposite? I mean of course something sensible, that is outside the sexual programme, free of resentment, illusion, and theory. Where is the man to be found capable of such superiority? Woman always stands just where the man's shadow falls, so that he is only too liable to confuse the two. Then, when he tries to repair this misunderstanding, he overvalues her and

---

1 [Originally published as "Die Frau in Europa," *Europäische Revue* (Berlin), III: 7 (Oct., 1927) ; republished by the *Neue Schweizer Rundschau* as a pamphlet (Zurich, 1929), which was reprinted by Rascher Verlag in 1932, 1948, and 1959 (cf. n. 2, infra). Trans. by C. F. and H. G. Baynes in *Contributions to Analytical Psychology* (London and New York, 1928), pp. 164–88, which version has been consulted here. The motto is from the trans. of Nietzsche by Common.—EDITORS.]

believes her the most desirable thing in the world. Thus it is with the greatest misgivings that I set out to treat of this theme.

237   One thing, however, is beyond doubt: that woman today is in the same process of transition as man. Whether this transition is a historical turning-point or not remains to be seen. Sometimes, when we look back at history, it seems as though the present time had analogies with certain periods in the past, when great empires and civilizations had passed their zenith and were hastening irresistibly towards decay. But these analogies are deceptive, for there are always renaissances. What *does* move more clearly into the foreground is Europe's position midway between the Asiatic East and the Anglo-Saxon—or shall we say American?—West. Europe now stands between two colossi, both uncouth in their form but implacably opposed to one another in their nature. They are profoundly different not only racially but in their ideals. In the West there is the maximum political freedom with the minimum personal freedom; in the East it is just the opposite. We see in the West a tremendous development of Europe's technological and scientific tendencies, and in the Far East an awakening of all those spiritual forces which, in Europe, these tendencies hold in check. The power of the West is material, that of the East ideal.[2] The struggle between these opposites, which in the world of the European man takes place in the realm of the scientifically applied intellect and finds expression on the battlefield and in the state of his bank balance, is, in woman, a psychic conflict.

238   What makes it so uncommonly difficult to discuss the problem of the modern European woman is that we are necessarily writing about a minority. There is no "modern European woman" properly speaking. Or is the peasant's wife of today different from her forbears of a hundred years ago? There is, in fact, a large body of the population that only to a very limited extent lives in the present and participates in present-day problems. We speak of a "woman's problem," but how many women have problems? In proportion to the sum-total of European women only a dwindling minority really live in the Europe of

[2] In the thirty years since this essay was written the significance of the "East" has changed and has largely assumed the form of the "Russian Empire." This already reaches as far as central Germany, but it has lost nothing of its Asiatic character. [Author's footnote in 1959 pamphlet edition.—EDITORS.]

today; and these are city dwellers and belong—to put it cautiously—to the more complicated of their kind. This must always be so, for it is only the few who clearly express the spirit of the present in any age. In the fourth and fifth centuries of our era there were only a very few Christians who in any way understood the spirit of Christianity, the rest were still practically pagan. The cultural process that is characteristic of an epoch operates most intensely in cities, for it needs large agglomerations of men to make civilization possible, and from these agglomerations culture gradually spreads to the smaller, backward groups. Thus we find the present only in the large centres, and there alone do we encounter the "European woman," the woman who expresses the social and spiritual aspect of contemporary Europe. The further we go from the influence of the great centres, the more we find ourselves receding into history. In the remote Alpine valleys we can meet people who have never seen a railway, and in Spain, which is also a part of Europe, we plunge to a dark medieval age lacking even an alphabet. The people of those regions, or of the corresponding social strata, do not live in our Europe but in the Europe of 1400, and their problems are those of the bygone age in which they dwell. I have analysed such people, and have found myself carried back into an ambience that was not wanting in historical romance.

39 The "present" is a thin surface stratum that is laid down in the great centres of civilization. If it is very thin, as in Tsarist Russia, it has no meaning, as events have shown. But once it has attained a certain strength, we can speak of civilization and progress, and then problems arise that are characteristic of an epoch. In this sense Europe has a present, and there are women who live in it and suffer its problems. About these, and these only, are we entitled to speak. Those who are satisfied with a medieval life have no need of the present and its experiments. But the man of the present cannot—no matter what the reason—turn back again to the past without suffering an essential loss. Often this turning back is altogether impossible, even if he were prepared to make the sacrifice. The man of the present must work for the future and leave others to conserve the past. He is therefore not only a builder but also a destroyer. He and his world have both become questionable and ambiguous. The

ways that the past shows him and the answers it gives to his questions are insufficient for the needs of the present. All the old, comfortable ways are blocked, new paths have been opened up, and new dangers have arisen of which the past knew nothing. It is proverbial that one never learns anything from history, and in regard to present-day problems it usually teaches us nothing. The new path has to be made through untrodden regions, without presuppositions and often, unfortunately, without piety. The only thing that cannot be improved upon is morality, for every alteration of traditional morality is by definition an immorality. This *bon mot* has an edge to it, against which many an innovator has barked his shins.

240   All the problems of the present form a tangled knot, and it is hardly possible to single out one particular problem and treat it independently of the others. Thus there is no problem of "woman in Europe" without man and his world. If she is married, she usually has to depend economically on her husband; if she is unmarried and earning a living, she is working in some profession designed by a man. Unless she is prepared to sacrifice her whole erotic life, she again stands in some essential relationship to man. In numerous ways woman is indissolubly bound up with man's world and is therefore just as exposed as he is to all the shocks of his world. The war, for instance, has affected woman just as profoundly as it has man, and she has to adapt to its consequences as he must. What the upheavals of the last twenty or thirty years mean for man's world is apparent to everyone; we can read about it every day in the newspapers. But what it means for woman is not so evident. Neither politically, nor economically, nor spiritually is she a factor of visible importance. If she were, she would loom more largely in man's field of vision and would have to be considered a rival. Sometimes she is seen in this role, but only as a man, so to speak, who is accidentally a woman. But since as a rule her place is on man's intimate side, the side of him that merely feels and has no eyes and does not want to see, woman appears as an impenetrable mask behind which everything possible and impossible can be conjectured—and actually seen!—without his getting anywhere near the mark. The elementary fact that a person always thinks another's psychology is identical with his own effectively prevents a correct understanding of feminine psychology. This is

abetted by woman's own unconsciousness and passivity, useful though these may be from the biological point of view: she allows herself to be convinced by the man's projected feelings. Of course this is a general human characteristic, but in woman it is given a particularly dangerous twist, because in this respect she is not naïve and it is only too often her *intention* to let herself be convinced by them. It fits in with her nature to keep her ego and her will in the background, so as not to hinder the man in any way, and to invite him to realize his intentions with regard to her person. This is a sexual pattern, but it has far-reaching ramifications in the feminine psyche. By maintaining a passive attitude with an ulterior purpose, she helps the man to realize his ends and in that way holds him. At the same time she is caught in her own toils, for whoever digs a pit for others falls into it himself.

41   I admit that this is a rather unkind description of a process which might well be sung in more lyrical strains. But all natural things have two sides, and when something has to be made conscious we must see the shadow side as well as the light.

42   When we observe the way in which women, since the second half of the nineteenth century, have begun to take up masculine professions, to become active in politics, to sit on committees, etc., we can see that woman is in the process of breaking with the purely feminine sexual pattern of unconsciousness and passivity, and has made a concession to masculine psychology by establishing herself as a visible member of society. She no longer hides behind the mask of Mrs. So-and-so, with the obliging intention of having all her wishes fulfilled by the man, or to make him pay for it if things do not go as she wishes.

43   This step towards social independence is a necessary response to economic and other factors, but in itself it is only a symptom and not the thing about which we are most concerned. Certainly the courage and capacity for self-sacrifice of such women is admirable, and only the blind could fail to see the good that has come out of all these efforts. But no one can get round the fact that by taking up a masculine profession, studying and working like a man, woman is doing something not wholly in accord with, if not directly injurious to, her feminine nature. She is doing something that would scarcely be possible for a man to do, unless he were a Chinese. Could he, for instance, be

a nursemaid or run a kindergarten? When I speak of injury, I do not mean merely physiological injury but above all psychic injury. It is a woman's outstanding characteristic that she can do anything for the love of a man. But those women who can achieve something important for the love of a *thing* are most exceptional, because this does not really agree with their nature. Love for a thing is a man's prerogative. But since masculine and feminine elements are united in our human nature, a man can live in the feminine part of himself, and a woman in her masculine part. None the less the feminine element in man is only something in the background, as is the masculine element in woman. If one lives out the opposite sex in oneself one is living in one's own background, and one's real individuality suffers. A man should live as a man and a woman as a woman. The contrasexual element in either sex is always dangerously close to the unconscious. It is even typical that the effects of the unconscious upon the conscious mind have a contrasexual character. For instance the soul (anima, psyche) has a feminine character which compensates the masculine consciousness. (Mystical instruction among primitives is exclusively a masculine concern, corresponding to the function of the Catholic priest.)

244   The immediate presence of the unconscious exerts a magnetic influence on the conscious processes. This explains the fear or even horror we have of the unconscious. It is a purposeful defence-reaction of the conscious mind. The contrasexual element has a mysterious charm tinged with fear, perhaps even with disgust. For this reason its charm is particularly attractive and fascinating, even when it comes to us not directly from outside, in the guise of a woman, but from within, as a psychic influence—for instance in the form of a temptation to abandon oneself to a mood or an affect. This example is not characteristic of women, for a woman's moods and emotions do not come to her directly from the unconscious but are peculiar to her feminine nature. They are therefore never naïve, but are mixed with an unacknowledged purpose. What comes to a woman from the unconscious is a sort of *opinion,* which spoils her mood only secondarily. These opinions lay claim to being absolute truths, and they prove to be the more fixed and incorrigible the less they are subjected to conscious criticism. Like the moods and feelings of a man, they are somewhat hazy and often

totally unconscious, and are seldom recognized for what they are. They are in fact collective, having the character of the opposite sex, as though a man—the father, for example—had thought of them.

245   Thus it can happen—indeed it is almost the rule—that the mind of a woman who takes up a masculine profession is influenced by her unconscious masculinity in a way not noticeable to herself but quite obvious to everybody in her environment. She develops a kind of rigid intellectuality based on so-called principles, and backs them up with a whole host of arguments which always just miss the mark in the most irritating way, and always inject a little something into the problem that is not really there. Unconscious assumptions or opinions are the worst enemy of woman; they can even grow into a positively demonic passion that exasperates and disgusts men, and does the woman herself the greatest injury by gradually smothering the charm and meaning of her femininity and driving it into the background. Such a development naturally ends in profound psychological disunion, in short, in a neurosis.

246   Naturally, things need not go to this length, but long before this point is reached the mental masculinization of the woman has unwelcome results. She may perhaps be a good comrade to a man without having any access to his feelings. The reason is that her animus (that is, her masculine rationalism, assuredly not true reasonableness!) has stopped up the approaches to her own feeling. She may even become frigid, as a defence against the masculine type of sexuality that corresponds to her masculine type of mind. Or, if the defence-reaction is not successful, she develops, instead of the receptive sexuality of woman, an aggressive, urgent form of sexuality that is more characteristic of a man. This reaction is likewise a purposeful phenomenon, intended to throw a bridge across by main force to the slowly vanishing man. A third possibility, especially favoured in Anglo-Saxon countries, is optional homosexuality in the masculine role.

247   It may therefore be said that, whenever the attraction of the animus becomes noticeable, there is a quite special need for the woman to have an intimate relationship with the other sex. Many women in this situation are fully aware of this necessity and proceed—*faute de mieux*—to stir up another of those

present-day problems that is no less painful, namely, the marriage problem.

248   Traditionally, man is regarded as the marriage breaker. This legend comes from times long past, when men still had leisure to pursue all sorts of pastimes. But today life makes so many demands on men that the noble hidalgo, Don Juan, is to be seen nowhere save in the theatre. More than ever man loves his comfort, for ours is an age of neurasthenia, impotence, and easy chairs. There is no energy left for window-climbing and duels. If anything is to happen in the way of adultery it must not be too difficult. In no respect must it cost too much, hence the adventure can only be of a transitory kind. The man of today is thoroughly scared of jeopardizing marriage as an institution. He is a firm believer in doing things on the quiet, and therefore supports prostitution. I would wager that in the Middle Ages, with its notorious bagnios and unrestricted prostitution, adultery was relatively more frequent than it is today. In this respect marriage should be safer now than it ever was. But in reality it is beginning to be discussed. It is a bad sign when doctors begin writing books of advice on how to achieve the "perfect marriage." Healthy people need no doctors. Marriage today has indeed become rather precarious. In America about a quarter of the marriages end in divorce. And the remarkable thing is that this time the scapegoat is not the man but the woman. She is the one who doubts and feels uncertain. It is not surprising that this is so, for in post-war Europe there is such an alarming surplus of unmarried women that it would be inconceivable if there were no reaction from that quarter. Such a piling up of misery has inescapable consequences. It is no longer a question of a few dozen voluntary or involuntary old maids here and there, but of millions. Our legislation and our social morality give no answer to this question. Or can the Church provide a satisfactory answer? Should we build gigantic nunneries to accommodate all these women? Or should tolerated prostitution be increased? Obviously this is impossible, since we are dealing neither with saints nor sinners but with ordinary women who cannot register their spiritual requirements with the police. They are decent women who want to marry, and if this is not possible, well—the next best thing. When it comes to the question of love, laws and institutions and ideals mean less to

woman than ever before. If things cannot go straight they will have to go crooked.

249   At the beginning of our era, three-fifths of the population of Italy consisted of slaves—human chattels without rights. Every Roman was surrounded by slaves. The slave and his psychology flooded ancient Italy, and every Roman became inwardly a slave. Living constantly in the atmosphere of slaves, he became infected with their psychology. No one can shield himself from this unconscious influence. Even today the European, however highly developed, cannot live with impunity among the Negroes in Africa; their psychology gets into him unnoticed and unconsciously he becomes a Negro. There is no fighting against it. In Africa there is a well-known technical expression for this: "going black." It is no mere snobbery that the English should consider anyone born in the colonies, even though the best blood may run in his veins, "slightly inferior." There are facts to support this view.

250   A direct result of slave influence was the strange melancholy and longing for deliverance that pervaded imperial Rome and found striking expression in Virgil's Fourth Eclogue. The explosive spread of Christianity, a religion which might be said to have risen from the sewers of Rome—Nietzsche called it a "slave insurrection in morals"—was a sudden reaction that set the soul of the lowest slave on a par with that of the divine Caesar. Similar though perhaps less momentous processes of psychological compensation have repeatedly occurred in the history of the world. Whenever some social or psychological monstrosity is created, a compensation comes along in defiance of all legislation and all expectation.

251   Something similar is happening to women in present-day Europe. Too much that is inadmissible, that has not been lived, is accumulating in the unconscious, and this is bound to have an effect. Secretaries, typists, shop-girls, all are agents of this process, and through a million subterranean channels creeps the influence that is undermining marriage. For the desire of all these women is not to have sexual adventures—only the stupid could believe that—but to get married. The possessors of that bliss must be ousted, not as a rule by naked force, but by that silent, obstinate desire which, as we know, has magical effects, like the fixed stare of a snake. This was ever the way of women.

252 What is the attitude of the married woman to all this? She clings to the old idea that man is the scapegoat, that he switches from one love-affair to another as he pleases, and so on. On the strength of these outworn conceptions she can wrap herself still more deeply in her jealousies. But all this is only on the surface. Neither the pride of the Roman patrician nor the thick walls of the imperial palace availed to keep out the slave infection. In the same way, no woman can escape the secret, compelling atmosphere with which her own sister, perhaps, is enveloping her, the stifling atmosphere of a life that has never been lived. Unlived life is a destructive, irresistible force that works softly but inexorably. The result is that the married woman begins to have doubts about marriage. The unmarried believe in it because they want it. Equally, the man believes in marriage because of his love of comfort and a sentimental belief in institutions, which for him always tend to become objects of feeling.

253 Since women have to be down to earth in matters of feeling, a certain fact should not escape our notice. This is the possibility of contraceptive measures. Children are one of the main reasons for maintaining a responsible attitude towards marriage. If this reason disappears, then the things that are "not done" happen easily enough. This applies primarily to unmarried women, who thus have an opportunity to contract an "approximate" marriage. But it is a consideration that counts also with all those married women who, as I have shown in my essay "Marriage as a Psychological Relationship," [3] are the "containers." By this I mean women whose demands as individuals are not satisfied, or not wholly satisfied, by their husbands. Finally, contraception is a fact of enormous importance to women in general, because it does away with the constant fear of pregnancy and the care of an ever-increasing number of children. This deliverance from bondage to nature brings a release of psychic energies that inevitably seek an outlet. Whenever a sum of energy finds no congenial goal it causes a disturbance of the psychic equilibrium. Lacking a conscious goal, it reinforces the unconscious and gives rise to uncertainty and doubt.

254 Another factor of great importance is the more or less open

[3] In *The Development of Personality, Coll. Works*, Vol. 17.

discussion of the sexual problem. This territory, once so obscure, has now become a focus of scientific and other interests. Things can be heard and said in society that formerly would have been quite impossible. Large numbers of people have learned to think more freely and honestly, and have come to realize how important these matters are. The discussion of the sexual problem is, however, only a somewhat crude prelude to a far deeper question, and that is the question of the psychological relationship between the sexes. In comparison with this the other pales into insignificance, and with it we enter the real domain of woman.

255   Woman's psychology is founded on the principle of Eros, the great binder and loosener, whereas from ancient times the ruling principle ascribed to man is Logos. The concept of Eros could be expressed in modern terms as psychic relatedness, and that of Logos as objective interest. In the eyes of the ordinary man, love in its true sense coincides with the institution of marriage, and outside marriage there is only adultery or "platonic" friendship. For woman, marriage is not an institution at all but a human love-relationship—at least that is what she would like to believe. (Since her Eros is not naïve but is mixed with other, unavowed motives—marriage as a ladder to social position, etc.—the principle cannot be applied in any absolute sense.) Marriage means to her an exclusive relationship. She can endure its exclusiveness all the more easily, without dying of ennui, inasmuch as she has children or near relatives with whom she has a no less intimate relationship than with her husband. The fact that she has no sexual relationship with these others means nothing, for the sexual relationship is of far less importance to her than the psychic relationship. It is enough that she and her husband both believe their relationship to be unique and exclusive. If he happens to be the "container" he feels suffocated by this exclusiveness, especially if he fails to notice that the exclusiveness of his wife is nothing but a pious fraud. In reality she is distributed among the children and among as many members of the family as possible, thus maintaining any number of intimate relationships. If her husband had anything like as many relationships with other people she would be mad with jealousy. Most men, though, are erotically blinded—they commit the unpardonable mistake of confusing

Eros with sex. A man thinks he possesses a woman if he has her sexually. He never possesses her less, for to a woman the Eros-relationship is the real and decisive one. For her, marriage is a relationship with sex thrown in as an accompaniment. Since sex is a formidable thing on account of its consequences, it is useful to have it in a safe place. But when it is less of a danger it also becomes less relevant, and then the question of relationship moves into the foreground.

256   It is just here that the woman runs into great difficulties with her husband, for the question of relationship borders on a region that for him is dark and painful. He can face this question only when the woman carries the burden of suffering, that is, when he is the "contained"—in other words, when she can imagine herself having a relationship with another man, and as a consequence suffering disunion within herself. Then it is she who has the painful problem, and he is not obliged to see his own, which is a great relief to him. In this situation he is not unlike a thief who, quite undeservedly, finds himself in the enviable position of having been forestalled by another thief who has been caught by the police. Suddenly he becomes an honourable, impartial onlooker. In any other situation a man always finds the discussion of personal relations painful and boring, just as his wife would find it boring if he examined her on the *Critique of Pure Reason*. For him, Eros is a shadow-land which entangles him in his feminine unconscious, in something "psychic," while for woman Logos is a deadly boring kind of sophistry if she is not actually repelled and frightened by it.

257   Just as woman began, towards the end of the nineteenth century, to make a concession to masculinity by taking her place as an independent factor in the social world, so man has made, somewhat hesitantly, a concession to femininity by creating a new psychology of complex phenomena, inaugurated by the sexual psychology of Freud. What this psychology owes to the direct influence of women—psychiatrists' consulting-rooms are packed with women—is a theme that would fill a large volume. I am speaking here not only of analytical psychology but of the beginnings of psychopathology in general. By far the greatest number of "classic" cases, beginning with the "Seeress of Prevorst," were women, who, perhaps unconsciously, took enor-

mous trouble to put their own psychology on view in the most dramatic fashion, and thus demonstrated to the world the whole question of psychic relationship. Women like Frau Hauffe and Hélène Smith [4] and Miss Beauchamp have assured for themselves a kind of immortality, rather like those worthy folk whose miraculous cures brought fame and prosperity to the wonder-working spot.

258   An astonishingly high percentage of this material comes from women. This is not as remarkable as it might seem, for women are far more "psychological" than men. A man is usually satisfied with "logic" alone. Everything "psychic," "unconscious" etc., is repugnant to him; he considers it vague, nebulous, and morbid. He is interested in things, in facts, and not in the feelings and fantasies that cluster round them or have nothing to do with them. To a woman it is generally more important to know how a man feels about a thing than to know the thing itself. All those things which are merely futile impedimenta to a man are important to her. So it is naturally woman who is the most direct exponent of psychology and gives it its richest content. Very many things can be perceived in her with the utmost distinctness which in a man are mere shadowy processes in the background, whose very existence he is unwilling to admit. But, unlike the objective discussion and verification of facts, a human relationship leads into the world of the psyche, into that intermediate realm between sense and spirit, which contains something of both and yet forfeits nothing of its own unique character.

259   Into this territory a man must venture if he wishes to meet woman half way. Circumstances have forced her to acquire a number of masculine traits, so that she shall not remain caught in an antiquated, purely instinctual femininity, lost and alone in the world of men. So, too, man will be forced to develop his feminine side, to open his eyes to the psyche and to Eros. It is a task he cannot avoid, unless he prefers to go trailing after woman in a hopelessly boyish fashion, worshipping from afar but always in danger of being stowed away in her pocket.

260   For those in love with masculinity or femininity *per se* the traditional medieval marriage is enough—and a thoroughly

4 [See *Psychiatric Studies, Coll. Works,* Vol. 1, index, s. vv.—EDITORS.]

praiseworthy, well-tried, useful institution it is. But the man of today finds it extremely difficult to return to it, and for many the way back is simply impossible, because this sort of marriage can exist only by shutting out all contemporary problems. Doubtless there were many Romans who could shut their eyes to the slave problem and to Christianity, and spend their days in a more or less pleasant unconsciousness. They could do this because they had no relation to the present, only to the past. All those for whom marriage contains no problem are not living in the present, and who shall say they are not blessed! Modern man finds marriage only too problematical. I recently heard a German scholar exclaim before an audience of several hundred people: "Our marriages are sham marriages!" I admired his courage and sincerity. Usually we express ourselves less directly, cautiously offering good advice as to what might be done—in order not to tarnish the ideal. But for the modern woman—let men take note of this—the medieval marriage is an ideal no longer. True, she keeps her doubts to herself, and hides her rebelliousness; one woman because she is married and finds it highly inconvenient if the door of the safe is not hermetically sealed, another because she is unmarried and too virtuous to look her own tendencies squarely in the face. Nevertheless, their newly-won masculinity makes it impossible for either of them to believe in marriage in its traditional form ("He shall be thy master"). Masculinity means knowing what one wants and doing what is necessary to achieve it. Once this lesson has been learned it is so obvious that it can never again be forgotten without tremendous psychic loss. The independence and critical judgment she acquires through this knowledge are positive values and are felt as such by the woman. She can never part with them again. The same is true of the man who, with great efforts, wins that needful feminine insight into his own psyche, often at the cost of much suffering. He will never let it go again, because he is thoroughly aware of the importance of what he has won.

261   At first glance it might be thought that such a man and woman would be especially likely to make the "perfect marriage." In reality this is not so; on the contrary, a conflict begins immediately. What the woman, in her new-found self-assurance, wants to do is not at all pleasing to the man, while the feelings

he has discovered in himself are far from agreeable to the woman. What both have discovered in themselves is not a virtue or anything of intrinsic value; it is something comparatively inferior, and it might justly be condemned if it were understood as the outcome of a personal choice or mood. And that, indeed, is what usually happens. The masculinity of the woman and the femininity of the man *are* inferior, and it is regrettable that the full value of their personalities should be contaminated by something that is less valuable. On the other hand, the shadow belongs to the wholeness of the personality: the strong man must somewhere be weak, somewhere the clever man must be stupid, otherwise he is too good to be true and falls back on pose and bluff. Is it not an old truth that woman loves the weaknesses of the strong man more than his strength, and the stupidity of the clever man more than his cleverness? Her love wants the whole man—not mere masculinity as such but also its negation. The love of woman is not sentiment, as is a man's, but a will that is at times terrifyingly unsentimental and can even force her to self-sacrifice. A man who is loved in this way cannot escape his inferior side, for he can only respond to the reality of her love with his own reality. And this reality is no fair semblance, but a faithful reflection of that eternal human nature which links together all humanity, a reflection of the heights and depths of human life which are common to us all. In this reality we are no longer differentiated persons (*persona* means a mask), but are conscious of our common human bonds. Here I strip off the distinctiveness of my own personality, social or otherwise, and reach down to the problems of the present day, problems which do not arise out of myself—or so at least I like to imagine. Here I can no longer deny them; I feel and know myself to be one of many, and what moves the many moves me. In our strength we are independent and isolated, and are masters of our own fate; in our weakness we are dependent and bound, and become unwilling instruments of fate, for here it is not the individual will that counts but the will of the species.

262   What the two sexes have won through mutual assimilation is an inferiority when viewed from the two-dimensional, personal world of appearances, and an immoral pretension if regarded as a personal claim. But in its truest meaning for life

and society it is an overcoming of personal isolation and selfish reserve in order to take an active part in the solution of present-day problems. If, therefore, the woman of today consciously or unconsciously loosens the cohesion of the marriage bond by her spiritual or economic independence, this is not the expression of her personal will, but of the will of the species, which makes her, the individual woman, its tool.

263   The institution of marriage is such a valuable thing, both socially and morally—religious people even regard it as a sacrament—that it is quite understandable that any weakening of it should be felt as undesirable, indeed scandalous. Human imperfection is always a discord in the harmony of our ideals. Unfortunately, no one lives in the world as we desire it, but in the world of actuality where good and evil clash and destroy one another, where no creating or building can be done without dirtying one's hands. Whenever things get really bad, there is always some one to assure us amid great applause that nothing has happened and everything is in order. I repeat, anyone who lives and thinks like this is not living in the present. If we examine any marriage with a really critical eye, we shall find—unless acute pressure of circumstances has completely extinguished all signs of "psychological" trouble—symptoms of its weakening and clandestine disruption, "marriage problems" ranging from unbearable moods to neurosis and adultery. Unfortunately, those who can still bear to remain unconscious cannot be imitated; their example is not infectious enough to induce more conscious people to descend again to the level of mere unconsciousness.

264   As to all those—and they are many—who are not obliged to live in the present, it is extremely important that they should believe in the ideal of marriage and hold fast to it. Nothing is gained if a valuable ideal is merely destroyed and not replaced by something better. Therefore even the women hesitate, whether they are married or not, to go over openly to the side of rebellion. But at least they do not follow the lead of that well-known authoress who, after trying out all sorts of experiments, ended up in the secure haven of matrimony, whereupon marriage became the best solution, and all those who did not achieve it could brood on their mistakes and end their days in pious renunciation. For the modern woman marriage is not as

easy as that. Her husband would have something to say on this score.

65   So long as there are legalistic clauses that lay down exactly what adultery is, women will have to remain with their doubts. But do our legislators really know what "adultery" is? Is their definition of it the final embodiment of the truth? From the psychological standpoint, the only one that counts for a woman, it is a wretched piece of bungling, like everything else contrived by men for the purpose of codifying love. For a woman, love has nothing to do with "marital misconduct," "extramarital intercourse," "deception of the husband," or any of the less savoury formulas invented by the erotically blind masculine intellect and echoed by the self-opinionated demon in woman. Nobody but the absolute believer in the inviolability of traditional marriage could perpetrate such breaches of good taste, just as only the believer in God can really blaspheme. Whoever doubts marriage in the first place cannot infringe against it; for him the legal definition is invalid because, like St. Paul, he feels himself beyond the law, on the higher plane of love. But because the believers in the law so frequently trespass against their own laws, whether from stupidity, temptation, or mere viciousness, the modern woman begins to wonder whether she too may not belong to the same category. From the traditional standpoint she does, and she has to realize this in order to smash the idol of her own respectability. To be "respectable" means, as the word tells us, to allow oneself to be seen; a respectable person is one who comes up to public expectations, who wears an ideal mask—in short, is a fraud. "Good form" is not a fraud, but when respectability represses the psyche, the God-given essence of man, then one becomes what Christ called a whited sepulchre.

66   The modern woman has become conscious of the undeniable fact that only in the state of love can she attain the highest and best of which she is capable, and this knowledge drives her to the other realization that love is beyond the law. Her respectability revolts against this, and one is inclined to identify this reaction with public opinion. That would be the lesser evil; what is worse is that public opinion is in her blood. It comes to her like a voice from within, a sort of conscience, and this is the power that holds her in check. She is unaware that love, her most personal, most prized possession, could bring her into

71

conflict with history. Such a thing would seem to her most unexpected and absurd. But who, if it comes to that, has fully realized that history is not contained in thick books but lives in our very blood?

267　So long as a woman lives the life of the past she can never come into conflict with history. But no sooner does she begin to deviate, however slightly, from a cultural trend that has dominated the past than she encounters the full weight of historical inertia, and this unexpected shock may injure her, perhaps fatally. Her hesitation and her doubt are understandable enough, for, if she submits to the law of love, she finds that she is not only in a highly disagreeable and dubious situation, where every kind of lewdness and depravity abounds, but actually caught between two universal forces—historical inertia and the divine urge to create.

268　Who, then, will blame her for hesitating? Do not most men prefer to rest on their laurels rather than get into a hopeless conflict as to whether they shall or shall not make history? In the end it boils down to this: is one prepared to break with tradition, to be "unhistorical" in order to make history, or not? No one can make history who is not willing to risk everything for it, to carry the experiment with his own life through to the bitter end, and to declare that his life is not a continuation of the past, but a new beginning. Mere continuation can be left to the animals, but inauguration is the prerogative of man, the one thing he can boast of that lifts him above the beasts.

269　There is no doubt that the woman of today is deeply concerned with this problem. She gives expression to one of the cultural tendencies of our time: the urge to live a completer life, a longing for meaning and fulfilment, a growing disgust with senseless one-sidedness, with unconscious instinctuality and blind contingency. The psyche of the modern European has not forgotten the lesson of the last war, however much it has been banished from his consciousness. Women are increasingly aware that love alone can give them full stature, just as men are beginning to divine that only the spirit can give life its highest meaning. Both seek a psychic relationship, because love needs the spirit, and the spirit love, for its completion.

270　Woman nowadays feels that there is no real security in marriage, for what does her husband's faithfulness mean when she knows that his feelings and thoughts are running after others and that he is merely too calculating or too cowardly to follow them? What does her own faithfulness mean when she knows that she is simply using it to exploit her legal right of possession, and warping her own soul? She has intimations of a higher fidelity to the spirit and to a love beyond human weakness and imperfection. Perhaps she will yet discover that what seems like weakness and imperfection, a painful disturbance, or an alarming deviation, must be interpreted in accordance with its dual nature. These are steps that lead down to the lowest human level and finally end in the morass of unconsciousness if the individual lets go of his personal distinctiveness. But if he can hold on to it, he will experience for the first time the meaning of selfhood, provided that he can simultaneously descend below himself into the undifferentiated mass of humanity. What else can free him from the inner isolation of his personal differentiation? And how else can he establish a psychic bridge to the rest of mankind? The man who stands on high and distributes his goods to the poor is separated from mankind by the height of his own virtue, and the more he forgets himself and sacrifices himself for others the more he is inwardly estranged from them.

271 The word "human" sounds very beautiful, but properly understood it does not mean anything particularly beautiful, or virtuous, or intelligent, but just a low average. This is the step which Zarathustra could not take, the step to the "Ugliest Man," who is real man. Our resistance to taking this step, and our fear of it, show how great is the attraction and seductive power of our own depths. To cut oneself off from them is no solution; it is a mere sham, an essential misunderstanding of their meaning and value. For where is a height without depth, and how can there be light that throws no shadow? There is no good that is not opposed by evil. "No man can be redeemed from a sin he has not committed," says Carpocrates; a deep saying for all who wish to understand, and a golden opportunity for all those who prefer to draw false conclusions. What is down below is not just an excuse for more pleasure, but something we fear because it demands to play its part in the life of the more conscious and more complete man.

73

272   What I am saying here is not for the young—it is precisely what they ought not to know—but for the more mature man whose consciousness has been widened by experience of life. No man can begin with the present; he must slowly grow into it, for there would be no present but for the past. A young person has not yet acquired a past, therefore he has no present either. He does not create culture, he merely exists. It is the privilege and the task of maturer people, who have passed the meridian of life, to create culture.

273   The European psyche has been torn to shreds by the hellish barbarism of the war. While man turns his hand to repairing the outer damage, woman—unconsciously as ever—sets about healing the inner wounds, and for this she needs, as her most important instrument, a psychic relationship. But nothing hampers this more than the exclusiveness of the medieval marriage, for it makes relationship altogether superfluous. Relationship is possible only if there is a psychic distance between people, in the same way that morality presupposes freedom. For this reason the unconscious tendency of woman aims at loosening the marriage structure, but not at the destruction of marriage and the family. That would be not only immoral but a thoroughly pathological misuse of her powers.

274   It would take volumes of case-material to describe the innumerable ways in which this goal is achieved. It is the way of woman, as of nature, to work indirectly, without naming her goal. To anything unsatisfactory she reacts purposively, with moods, outbursts of affects, opinions, and actions that all have the same end in view, and their apparent senselessness, virulence, and cold-blooded ruthlessness are infinitely distressing to the man who is blind to Eros.

275   The indirect method of woman is dangerous, for it can hopelessly compromise her aim. That is why she longs for greater consciousness, which would enable her to name her goal and give it meaning, and thus escape the blind dynamism of nature. In any other age it would have been the prevailing religion that showed her where her ultimate goal lay; but today religion leads back to the Middle Ages, back to that soul-destroying unrelatedness from which came all the fearful barbarities of war. Too much soul is reserved for God, too little for man. But God

74

himself cannot flourish if man's soul is starved. The feminine psyche responds to this hunger, for it is the function of Eros to unite what Logos has sundered. The woman of today is faced with a tremendous cultural task—perhaps it will be the dawn of a new era.

ANIMA AND ANIMUS

296   Among all possible spirits the spirits of the parents are in practice the most important; hence the universal incidence of the ancestor cult. In its original form it served to conciliate the *revenants,* but on a higher level of culture it became an essentially moral and educational institution, as in China. For the child, the parents are his closest and most influential relations. But as he grows older this influence is split off; consequently the parental imagos become increasingly shut away from consciousness, and on account of the restrictive influence they sometimes continue to exert, they easily acquire a negative aspect. In this way the parental imagos remain as alien elements somewhere "outside" the psyche. In place of the parents, woman now takes up her position as the most immediate environmental influence in the life of the adult man. She becomes his companion, she belongs to him in so far as she shares his life and is more or less of the same age. She is not of a superior order, either by virtue of age, authority, or physical strength. She is, however, a very influential factor and, like the parents, she produces an imago of a relatively autonomous nature—not an imago to be split off like that of the parents, but one that has to be kept associated with consciousness. Woman, with her very dissimilar psychology, is and always has been a source of information about things for which a man has no eyes. She can be his inspiration; her intuitive capacity, often superior to man's, can give him timely warning, and her feeling, always directed towards the personal, can show him ways which his own less personally accented feeling would never have discovered. What Tacitus says about the Germanic women is exactly to the point in this respect.[1]

297   Here, without a doubt, is one of the main sources for the feminine quality of the soul. But it does not seem to be the only

1 *Germania* (Loeb edn.), pars. 18, 19.

77

source. No man is so entirely masculine that he has nothing feminine in him. The fact is, rather, that very masculine men have—carefully guarded and hidden—a very soft emotional life, often incorrectly described as "feminine." A man counts it a virtue to repress his feminine traits as much as possible, just as a woman, at least until recently, considered it unbecoming to be "mannish." The repression of feminine traits and inclinations naturally causes these contrasexual demands to accumulate in the unconscious. No less naturally, the imago of woman (the soul-image) becomes a receptacle for these demands, which is why a man, in his love-choice, is strongly tempted to win the woman who best corresponds to his own unconscious femininity—a woman, in short, who can unhesitatingly receive the projection of his soul. Although such a choice is often regarded and felt as altogether ideal, it may turn out that the man has manifestly married his own worst weakness. This would explain some highly remarkable conjunctions.

298   It seems to me, therefore, that apart from the influence of woman there is also the man's own femininity to explain the feminine nature of the soul-complex. There is no question here of any linguistic "accident," of the kind that makes the sun feminine in German and masculine in other languages. We have, in this matter, the testimony of art from all ages, and besides that the famous question: *habet mulier animam?* Most men, probably, who have any psychological insight at all will know what Rider Haggard means by "She-who-must-be-obeyed," and will also recognize the chord that is struck when they read Benoît's description of Antinéa.[2] Moreover they know at once the kind of woman who most readily embodies this mysterious factor, of which they have so vivid a premonition.

299   The wide recognition accorded to such books shows that there must be some supra-individual quality in this image of the anima,[3] something that does not owe a fleeting existence simply to its individual uniqueness, but is far more typical, with roots that go deeper than the obvious surface attachments I have pointed out. Both Rider Haggard and Benoît give unmistak-

2 Cf. Rider Haggard, *She;* Benoît, *L'Atlantide.*
3 Cf. *Psychological Types,* Def. 48, "Soul." [Also "Concerning the Archetypes, with Special Reference to the Anima Concept" and "The Psychological Aspects of the Kore."—EDITORS.]

able utterance to this supposition in the *historical* aspect of their anima figures.

300   As we know, there is no human experience, nor would experience be possible at all, without the intervention of a subjective aptitude. What is this subjective aptitude? Ultimately it consists in an innate psychic structure which allows man to have experiences of this kind. Thus the whole nature of man presupposes woman, both physically and spiritually. His system is tuned in to woman from the start, just as it is prepared for a quite definite world where there is water, light, air, salt, carbohydrates, etc. The form of the world into which he is born is already inborn in him as a virtual image. Likewise parents, wife, children, birth, and death are inborn in him as virtual images, as psychic aptitudes. These *a priori* categories have by nature a collective character; they are images of parents, wife, and children in general, and are not individual predestinations. We must therefore think of these images as lacking in solid content, hence as unconscious. They only acquire solidity, influence, and eventual consciousness in the encounter with empirical facts, which touch the unconscious aptitude and quicken it to life. They are in a sense the deposits of all our ancestral experiences, but they are not the experiences themselves. So at least it seems to us, in the present limited state of our knowledge. (I must confess that I have never yet found infallible evidence for the inheritance of memory images, but I do not regard it as positively precluded that in addition to these collective deposits which contain nothing specifically individual, there may also be inherited memories that are individually determined.)

301   An inherited collective image of woman exists in a man's unconscious, with the help of which he apprehends the nature of woman. This inherited image is the third important source for the femininity of the soul.

302   As the reader will have grasped, we are not concerned here with a philosophical, much less a religious, concept of the soul, but with the psychological recognition of the existence of a semiconscious psychic complex, having partial autonomy of function. Clearly, this recognition has as much or as little to do with philosophical or religious conceptions of the soul, as psychology has as much or as little to do with philosophy or religion. I have no wish to embark here on a "battle of the facul-

79

ties," nor do I seek to demonstrate either to the philosopher or to the theologian what exactly he means by "soul." I must, however, restrain both of them from prescribing what the psychologist *ought* to mean by "soul." The quality of personal immortality so fondly attributed to the soul by religion is, for science, no more than a psychological *indicium* which is already included in the idea of autonomy. The quality of personal immortality is by no means a constant attribute of the soul as the primitive sees it, nor even immortality as such. But setting this view aside as altogether inaccessible to science, the immediate meaning of "immortality" is simply a psychic activity that transcends the limits of consciousness. "Beyond the grave" or "on the other side of death" means, psychologically, "beyond consciousness." There is positively nothing else it could mean, since statements about immortality can only be made by the living, who, as such, are not exactly in a position to pontificate about conditions "beyond the grave."

303   The autonomy of the soul-complex naturally lends support to the notion of an invisible, personal entity that apparently lives in a world very different from ours. Consequently, once the activity of the soul is felt to be that of an autonomous entity having no ties with our mortal substance, it is but a step to imagining that this entity must lead an entirely independent existence, perhaps in a world of invisible things. Yet it is not immediately clear why the *invisibility* of this independent entity should simultaneously imply its *immortality*. The quality of immortality might easily derive from another fact to which I have already alluded, namely the characteristically historical aspect of the soul. Rider Haggard has given one of the best descriptions of this in *She*. When the Buddhists say that progressive perfection through meditation awakens memories of former incarnations, they are no doubt referring to the same psychological reality, the only difference being that they ascribe the historical factor not to the soul but to the Self (*atman*). It is altogether in keeping with the thoroughly extraverted attitude of the Western mind so far, that immortality should be ascribed, both by feeling and by tradition, to a soul which we distinguish more or less from our ego, and which also differs from the ego on account of its feminine qualities. It would be entirely logical if, by deepening that neglected, introverted side of our spiritual culture, there

were to take place in us a transformation more akin to the Eastern frame of mind, where the quality of immortality would transfer itself from the ambiguous figure of the soul (*anima*) to the self. For it is essentially the overvaluation of the material object without that constellates a spiritual and immortal figure within (obviously for the purpose of compensation and self-regulation). Fundamentally, the historical factor does not attach only to the archetype of the feminine, but to all archetypes whatsoever, i.e., to every inherited unit, mental as well as physical. Our life is indeed the same as it ever was. At all events, in our sense of the word it is not transitory; for the same physiological and psychological processes that have been man's for hundreds of thousands of years still endure, instilling into our inmost hearts this profound intuition of the "eternal" continuity of the living. But the self, as an inclusive term that embraces our whole living organism, not only contains the deposit and totality of all past life, but is also a point of departure, the fertile soil from which all future life will spring. This premonition of futurity is as clearly impressed upon our innermost feelings as is the historical aspect. The idea of immortality follows legitimately from these psychological premises.

304   In the Eastern view the concept of the anima, as we have stated it here, is lacking, and so, logically, is the concept of a persona. This is certainly no accident, for, as I have already indicated, a compensatory relationship exists between persona and anima.

305   The persona is a complicated system of relations between the individual consciousness and society, fittingly enough a kind of mask, designed on the one hand to make a definite impression upon others, and, on the other, to conceal the true nature of the individual. That the latter function is superfluous could be maintained only by one who is so identified with his persona that he no longer knows himself; and that the former is unnecessary could only occur to one who is quite unconscious of the true nature of his fellows. Society expects, and indeed must expect, every individual to play the part assigned to him as perfectly as possible, so that a man who is a parson must not only carry out his official functions objectively, but must at all times and in all circumstances play the role of parson in a flawless manner. Society demands this as a kind of surety; each must stand at his

post, here a cobbler, there a poet. No man is expected to be both. Nor is it advisable to be both, for that would be "odd." Such a man would be "different" from other people, not quite reliable. In the academic world he would be a dilettante, in politics an "unpredictable" quantity, in religion a free-thinker—in short, he would always be suspected of unreliability and incompetence, because society is persuaded that only the cobbler who is not a poet can supply workmanlike shoes. To present an unequivocal face to the world is a matter of practical importance: the average man—the only kind society knows anything about—must keep his nose to one thing in order to achieve anything worth while, two would be too much. Our society is undoubtedly set on such an ideal. It is therefore not surprising that everyone who wants to get on must take these expectations into account. Obviously no one could completely submerge his individuality in these expectations; hence the construction of an artificial personality becomes an unavoidable necessity. The demands of propriety and good manners are an added inducement to assume a becoming mask. What goes on behind the mask is then called "private life." This painfully familiar division of consciousness into two figures, often preposterously different, is an incisive psychological operation that is bound to have repercussions on the unconscious.

306   The construction of a collectively suitable persona means a formidable concession to the external world, a genuine self-sacrifice which drives the ego straight into identification with the persona, so that people really do exist who believe they are what they pretend to be. The "soullessness" of such an attitude is, however, only apparent, for under no circumstances will the unconscious tolerate this shifting of the centre of gravity. When we examine such cases critically, we find that the excellence of the mask is compensated by the "private life" going on behind it. The pious Drummond once lamented that "bad temper is the vice of the virtuous." Whoever builds up too good a persona for himself naturally has to pay for it with irritability. Bismarck had hysterical weeping fits, Wagner indulged in correspondence about the belts of silk dressing-gowns, Nietzsche wrote letters to his "dear lama," Goethe held conversations with Eckermann, etc. But there are subtler things than the banal lapses of heroes. I once made the acquaintance of a very venerable personage—in

fact, one might easily call him a saint. I stalked round him for three whole days, but never a mortal failing did I find in him. My feeling of inferiority grew ominous, and I was beginning to think seriously of how I might better myself. Then, on the fourth day, his wife came to consult me. . . . Well, nothing of the sort has ever happened to me since. But this I did learn: that any man who becomes one with his persona can cheerfully let all disturbances manifest themselves through his wife without her noticing it, though she pays for her self-sacrifice with a bad neurosis.

307 These identifications with a social role are a very fruitful source of neuroses. A man cannot get rid of himself in favour of an artificial personality without punishment. Even the attempt to do so brings on, in all ordinary cases, unconscious reactions in the form of bad moods, affects, phobias, obsessive ideas, backslidings, vices, etc. The social "strong man" is in his private life often a mere child where his own states of feeling are concerned; his discipline in public (which he demands quite particularly of others) goes miserably to pieces in private. His "happiness in his work" assumes a woeful countenance at home; his "spotless" public morality looks strange indeed behind the mask—we will not mention deeds, but only fantasies, and the wives of such men would have a pretty tale to tell. As to his selfless altruism, his children have decided views about that.

308 To the degree that the world invites the individual to identify with the mask, he is delivered over to influences from within. "High rests on low," says Lao-tzu. An opposite forces its way up from inside; it is exactly as though the unconscious suppressed the ego with the very same power which drew the ego into the persona. The absence of resistance outwardly against the lure of the persona means a similar weakness inwardly against the influence of the unconscious. Outwardly an effective and powerful role is played, while inwardly an effeminate weakness develops in face of every influence coming from the unconscious. Moods, vagaries, timidity, even a limp sexuality (culminating in impotence) gradually gain the upper hand.

309 The persona, the ideal picture of a man as he should be, is inwardly compensated by feminine weakness, and as the individual outwardly plays the strong man, so he becomes inwardly a woman, i.e., the anima, for it is the anima that reacts to the

persona. But because the inner world is dark and invisible to the extraverted consciousness, and because a man is all the less capable of conceiving his weaknesses the more he is identified with the persona, the persona's counterpart, the anima, remains completely in the dark and is at once projected, so that our hero comes under the heel of his wife's slipper. If this results in a considerable increase of her power, she will acquit herself none too well. She becomes inferior, thus providing her husband with the welcome proof that it is not he, the hero, who is inferior in private, but his wife. In return the wife can cherish the illusion, so attractive to many, that at least she has married a hero, unperturbed by her own uselessness. This little game of illusion is often taken to be the whole meaning of life.

310   Just as, for the purpose of individuation, or self-realization, it is essential for a man to distinguish between what he is and how he appears to himself and to others, so it is also necessary for the same purpose that he should become conscious of his invisible system of relations to the unconscious, and especially of the anima, so as to be able to distinguish himself from her. One cannot of course distinguish oneself from something unconscious. In the matter of the persona it is easy enough to make it clear to a man that he and his office are two different things. But it is very difficult for a man to distinguish himself from his anima, the more so because she is invisible. Indeed, he has first to contend with the prejudice that everything coming from inside him springs from the truest depths of his being. The "strong man" will perhaps concede that in private life he is singularly undisciplined, but that, he says, is just his "weakness" with which, as it were, he proclaims his solidarity. Now there is in this tendency a cultural legacy that is not to be despised; for when a man recognizes that his ideal persona is responsible for his anything but ideal anima, his ideals are shattered, the world becomes ambiguous, he becomes ambiguous even to himself. He is seized by doubts about goodness, and what is worse, he doubts his own good intentions. When one considers how much our private idea of good intentions is bound up with vast historical assumptions, it will readily be understood that it is pleasanter and more in keeping with our present view of the world to deplore a personal weakness than to shatter ideals.

311   But since the unconscious factors act as determinants no less

84

than the factors that regulate the life of society, and are no less collective, I might just as well learn to distinguish between what *I* want and what the unconscious thrusts upon me, as to see what my office demands of me and what I myself desire. At first the only thing that is at all clear is the incompatibility of the demands coming from without and from within, with the ego standing between them, as between hammer and anvil. But over against this ego, tossed like a shuttlecock between the outer and inner demands, there stands some scarcely definable arbiter, which I would on no account label with the deceptive name "conscience," although, taken in its best sense, the word fits that arbiter very aptly indeed. What we have made of this "conscience" Spitteler has described with unsurpassable humour.[4] Hence we should strenuously avoid this particular signification. We should do far better to realize that the tragic counterplay between inside and outside (depicted in Job and *Faust* as the wager with God) represents, at bottom, the energetics of the life process, the polar tension that is necessary for self-regulation. However different, to all intents and purposes, these opposing forces may be, their fundamental meaning and desire is the life of the individual: they always fluctuate round this centre of balance. Just because they are inseparably related through opposition, they also unite in a mediatory meaning, which, willingly or unwillingly, is born out of the individual and is therefore divined by him. He has a strong feeling of what should be and what could be. To depart from this divination means error, aberration, illness.

312   It is probably no accident that our modern notions of "personal" and "personality" derive from the word *persona*. I can assert that my ego is personal or a personality, and in exactly the same sense I can say that my persona is a personality with which I identify myself more or less. The fact that I then possess two personalities is not so remarkable, since every autonomous or even relatively autonomous complex has the peculiarity of appearing as a personality, i.e., of being personified. This can be observed most readily in the so-called spiritualistic manifestations of automatic writing and the like. The sentences produced are always personal statements and are propounded in the first person singular, as though behind every utterance there stood

[4] *Psychological Types*, pars. 282ff.

an actual personality. A naïve intelligence at once thinks of spirits. The same sort of thing is also observable in the hallucinations of the insane, although these, more clearly than the first, can often be recognized as mere thoughts or fragments of thoughts whose connection with the conscious personality is immediately apparent to everyone.

3   The tendency of the relatively autonomous complex to direct personification also explains why the persona exercises such a "personal" effect that the ego is all too easily deceived as to which is the "true" personality.

4   Now, everything that is true of the persona and of all autonomous complexes in general also holds true of the anima. She likewise is a personality, and this is why she is so easily projected upon a woman. So long as the anima is unconscious she is always projected, for everything unconscious is projected. The first bearer of the soul-image is always the mother; later it is borne by those women who arouse the man's feelings, whether in a positive or a negative sense. Because the mother is the first bearer of the soul-image, separation from her is a delicate and important matter of the greatest educational significance. Accordingly among primitives we find a large number of rites designed to organize this separation. The mere fact of becoming adult, and of outward separation, is not enough; impressive initiations into the "men's house" and ceremonies of rebirth are still needed in order to make the separation from the mother (and hence from childhood) entirely effective.

15   Just as the father acts as a protection against the dangers of the external world and thus serves his son as a model persona, so the mother protects him against the dangers that threaten from the darkness of his psyche. In the puberty rites, therefore, the initiate receives instruction about these things of "the other side," so that he is put in a position to dispense with his mother's protection.

16   The modern civilized man has to forgo this primitive but nonetheless admirable system of education. The consequence is that the anima, in the form of the mother-imago, is transferred to the wife; and the man, as soon as he marries, becomes childish, sentimental, dependent, and subservient, or else truculent, tyrannical, hypersensitive, always thinking about the prestige of his superior masculinity. The last is of course merely the reverse

of the first. The safeguard against the unconscious, which is what his mother meant to him, is not replaced by anything in the modern man's education; unconsciously, therefore, his ideal of marriage is so arranged that his wife has to take over the magical role of the mother. Under the cloak of the ideally exclusive marriage he is really seeking his mother's protection, and thus he plays into the hands of his wife's possessive instincts. His fear of the dark incalculable power of the unconscious gives his wife an illegitimate authority over him, and forges such a dangerously close union that the marriage is permanently on the brink of explosion from internal tension—or else, out of protest, he flies to the other extreme, with the same results.

317   I am of the opinion that it is absolutely essential for a certain type of modern man to recognize his distinction not only from the persona, but from the anima as well. For the most part our consciousness, in true Western style, looks outwards, and the inner world remains in darkness. But this difficulty can be overcome easily enough, if only we will make the effort to apply the same concentration and criticism to the psychic material which manifests itself, not outside, but in our private lives. So accustomed are we to keep a shamefaced silence about this other side—we even tremble before our wives, lest they betray us!—and, if found out, to make rueful confessions of "weakness," that there would seem to be only one method of education, namely, to crush or repress the weaknesses as much as possible or at least hide them from the public. But that gets us nowhere.

318   Perhaps I can best explain what has to be done if I use the persona as an example. Here everything is plain and straightforward, whereas with the anima all is dark, to Western eyes anyway. When the anima continually thwarts the good intentions of the conscious mind, by contriving a private life that stands in sorry contrast to the dazzling persona, it is exactly the same as when a naive individual, who has not the ghost of a persona, encounters the most painful difficulties in his passage through the world. There are indeed people who lack a developed persona—"Canadians who know not Europe's sham politeness"—blundering from one social solecism to the next, perfectly harmless and innocent, soulful bores or appealing children, or, if they are women, spectral Cassandras dreaded for their tactlessness, eternally misunderstood, never knowing what they are about, al-

ways taking forgiveness for granted, blind to the world, hopeless dreamers. From them we can see how a neglected persona works, and what one must do to remedy the evil. Such people can avoid disappointments and an infinity of sufferings, scenes, and social catastrophes only by learning to see how men behave in the world. They must learn to understand what society expects of them; they must realize that there are factors and persons in the world far above them; they must know that what they do has a meaning for others, and so forth. Naturally all this is child's play for one who has a properly developed persona. But if we reverse the picture and confront the man who possesses a brilliant persona with the anima, and, for the sake of comparison, set him beside the man with no persona, then we shall see that the latter is just as well informed about the anima and her affairs as the former is about the world. The use which either makes of his knowledge can just as easily be abused, in fact it is more than likely that it will be.

319   The man with the persona is blind to the existence of inner realities, just as the other is blind to the reality of the world, which for him has merely the value of an amusing or fantastic playground. But the fact of inner realities and their unqualified recognition is obviously the *sine qua non* for a serious consideration of the anima problem. If the external world is, for me, simply a phantasm, how should I take the trouble to establish a complicated system of relationship and adaptation to it? Equally, the "nothing but fantasy" attitude will never persuade me to regard my anima manifestations as anything more than fatuous weakness. If, however, I take the line that the world is outside *and* inside, that reality falls to the share of both, I must logically accept the upsets and annoyances that come to me from inside as symptoms of faulty adaptation to the conditions of that inner world. No more than the blows rained on the innocent abroad can be healed by moral repression will it help him resignedly to catalogue his "weaknesses." Here are reasons, intentions, consequences, which can be tackled by will and understanding. Take, for example, the "spotless" man of honour and public benefactor, whose tantrums and explosive moodiness terrify his wife and children. What is the anima doing here?

320   We can see it at once if we just allow things to take their natural course. Wife and children will become estranged; a vac-

uum will form about him. At first he will bewail the hard-heartedness of his family, and will behave if possible even more vilely than before. That will make the estrangement absolute. If the good spirits have not utterly forsaken him, he will after a time notice his isolation, and in his loneliness he will begin to understand how he caused the estrangement. Perhaps, aghast at himself, he will ask, "What sort of devil has got into me?"—without of course seeing the meaning of this metaphor. Then follow remorse, reconciliation, oblivion, repression, and, in next to no time, a new explosion. Clearly, the anima is trying to enforce a separation. This tendency is in nobody's interest. The anima comes between them like a jealous mistress who tries to alienate the man from his family. An official post or any other advantageous social position can do the same thing, but there we can understand the force of the attraction. Whence does the anima obtain the power to wield such enchantment? On the analogy with the persona there must be values or some other important and influential factors lying in the background like seductive promises. In such matters we must guard against rationalizations. Our first thought is that the man of honour is on the look-out for another woman. That might be—it might even be arranged by the anima as the most effective means to the desired end. Such an arrangement should not be misconstrued as an end in itself, for the blameless gentleman who is correctly married according to the law can be just as correctly divorced according to the law, which does not alter his fundamental attitude one iota. The old picture has merely received a new frame.

21   As a matter of fact, this arrangement is a very common method of implementing a separation—and of hampering a final solution. Therefore it is more reasonable not to assume that such an obvious possibility is the end-purpose of the separation. We would be better advised to investigate what is behind the tendencies of the anima. The first step is what I would call the objectivation of the anima, that is, the strict refusal to regard the trend towards separation as a weakness of one's own. Only when this has been done can one face the anima with the question, "Why do you want this separation?" To put the question in this personal way has the great advantage of recognizing the anima as a personality, and of making a relationship possible. The more personally she is taken the better.

322   To anyone accustomed to proceed purely intellectually and rationally, this may seem altogether too ridiculous. It would indeed be the height of absurdity if a man tried to have a conversation with his persona, which he recognized merely as a psychological means of relationship. But it is absurd only for the man who *has* a persona. If he has none, he is in this point no different from the primitive who, as we know, has only one foot in what we commonly call reality. With the other foot he stands in a world of spirits, which is quite real to him. Our model case behaves, in the world, like a modern European; but in the world of spirits he is the child of a troglodyte. He must therefore submit to living in a kind of prehistoric kindergarten until he has got the right idea of the powers and factors which rule that other world. Hence he is quite right to treat the anima as an autonomous personality and to address personal questions to her. •

323   I mean this as an actual technique. We know that practically every one has not only the peculiarity, but also the faculty, of holding a conversation with himself. Whenever we are in a predicament we ask ourselves (or whom else?), "What shall I do?" either aloud or beneath our breath, and we (or who else?) supply the answer. Since it is our intention to learn what we can about the foundations of our being, this little matter of living in a metaphor should not bother us. We have to accept it as a symbol of our primitive backwardness (or of such naturalness as is still, mercifully, left to us) that we can, like the Negro, discourse personally with our "snake." The psyche not being a unity but a contradictory multiplicity of complexes, the dissociation required for our dialectics with the anima is not so terribly difficult. The art of it consists only in allowing our invisible partner to make herself heard, in putting the mechanism of expression momentarily at her disposal, without being overcome by the distaste one naturally feels at playing such an apparently ludicrous game with oneself, or by doubts as to the genuineness of the voice of one's interlocutor. This latter point is technically very important: we are so in the habit of identifying ourselves with the thoughts that come to us that we invariably assume we have made them. Curiously enough, it is precisely the most impossible thoughts for which we feel the greatest subjective responsibility. If we were more conscious of the inflexible universal laws that govern even the wildest and most wanton fantasy, we

might perhaps be in a better position to see these thoughts above all others as objective occurrences, just as we see dreams, which nobody supposes to be deliberate or arbitrary inventions. It certainly requires the greatest objectivity and absence of prejudice to give the "other side" the opportunity for perceptible psychic activity. As a result of the repressive attitude of the conscious mind, the other side is driven into indirect and purely symptomatic manifestations, mostly of an emotional kind, and only in moments of overwhelming affectivity can fragments of the unconscious come to the surface in the form of thoughts or images. The inevitable accompanying symptom is that the ego momentarily identifies with these utterances, only to revoke them in the same breath. And, indeed, the things one says when in the grip of an affect sometimes seem very strange and daring. But they are easily forgotten, or wholly denied. This mechanism of deprecation and denial naturally has to be reckoned with if one wants to adopt an objective attitude. The habit of rushing in to correct and criticize is already strong enough in our tradition, and it is as a rule further reinforced by fear—a fear that can be confessed neither to oneself nor to others, a fear of insidious truths, of dangerous knowledge, of disagreeable verifications, in a word, fear of all those things that cause so many of us to flee from being alone with ourselves as from the plague. We say that it is egoistic or "morbid" to be preoccupied with oneself; one's own company is the worst, "it makes you melancholy"—such are the glowing testimonials accorded to our human make-up. They are evidently deeply ingrained in our Western minds. Whoever thinks in this way has obviously never asked himself what possible pleasure other people could find in the company of such a miserable coward. Starting from the fact that in a state of affect one often surrenders involuntarily to the truths of the other side, would it not be far better to make use of an affect so as to give the other side an opportunity to speak? It could therefore be said just as truly that one should cultivate the art of conversing with oneself in the setting provided by an affect, as though the affect itself were speaking without regard to our rational criticism. So long as the affect is speaking, criticism must be withheld. But once it has presented its case, we should begin criticizing as conscientiously as though a real person closely connected with us were our interlocutor. Nor should the matter rest there, but statement and answer must follow one another until a satisfactory end to the discussion is reached. Whether the result is satisfactory or not, only subjective feeling can decide. Any humbug is of course quite useless. Scrupulous honesty with oneself and no rash anticipation of what the other side might conceivably say are the indispensable conditions of this technique for educating the anima.

324   There is, however, something to be said for this characteristically Western fear of the other side. It is not entirely without justification, quite apart from the fact that it is real. We can understand at once the fear that the child and the primitive have of the great unknown. We have the same childish fear of our inner side, where we likewise touch upon a great unknown world. All we have is the affect, the fear, without knowing that this is a world-fear—for the world of affects is invisible. We have either purely theoretical prejudices against it, or superstitious ideas. One cannot even talk about the unconscious before many educated people without being accused of mysticism. The fear is legitimate in so far as our rational *Weltanschauung* with its scientific and moral certitudes—so hotly believed in because so deeply questionable—is shattered by the facts of the other side. If only one could avoid them, then the emphatic advice of the Philistine to "let sleeping dogs lie" would be the only truth worth advocating. And here I would expressly point out that I am not recommending the above technique as either necessary or even useful to any person not driven to it by necessity. The stages, as I said, are many, and there are greybeards who die as innocent as babes in arms, and in this year of grace troglodytes are still being born. There are truths which belong to the future, truths which belong to the past, and truths which belong to no time.

325   I can imagine someone using this technique out of a kind of holy inquisitiveness, some youth, perhaps, who would like to set wings to his feet, not because of lameness, but because he yearns for the sun. But a grown man, with too many illusions dissipated, will submit to this inner humiliation and surrender only if forced, for why should he let the terrors of childhood again have their way with him? It is no light matter to stand between a day-world of exploded ideals and discredited values, and a night-world of apparently senseless fantasy. The weirdness of this

standpoint is in fact so great that there is probably nobody who does not reach out for security, even though it be a reaching back to the mother who shielded his childhood from the terrors of night. Whoever is afraid must needs be dependent; a weak thing needs support. That is why the primitive mind, from deep psychological necessity, begot religious instruction and embodied it in magician and priest. *Extra ecclesiam nulla salus* is still a valid truth today—for those who can go back to it. For the few who cannot, there is only dependence upon a human being, a humbler and a prouder dependence, a weaker and a stronger support, so it seems to me, than any other. What can one say of the Protestant? He has neither church nor priest, but only God—and even God becomes doubtful.

326   The reader may ask in some consternation, "But what on earth does the anima do, that such double insurances are needed before one can come to terms with her?" I would recommend my reader to study the comparative history of religion so intently as to fill these dead chronicles with the emotional life of those who lived these religions. Then he will get some idea of what lives on the other side. The old religions with their sublime and ridiculous, their friendly and fiendish symbols did not drop from the blue, but were born of this human soul that dwells within us at this moment. All those things, their primal forms, live on in us and may at any time burst in upon us with annihilating force, in the guise of mass-suggestions against which the individual is defenceless. Our fearsome gods have only changed their names: they now rhyme with *ism.* Or has anyone the nerve to claim that the World War or Bolshevism was an ingenious invention? Just as outwardly we live in a world where a whole continent may be submerged at any moment, or a pole be shifted, or a new pestilence break out, so inwardly we live in a world where at any moment something similar may occur, albeit in the form of an idea, but no less dangerous and untrustworthy for that. Failure to adapt to this inner world is a negligence entailing just as serious consequences as ignorance and ineptitude in the outer world. It is after all only a tiny fraction of humanity, living mainly on that thickly populated peninsula of Asia which juts out into the Atlantic Ocean, and calling themselves "cultured," who, because they lack all contact with nature, have hit upon the idea that religion is a peculiar kind of

mental disturbance of undiscoverable purport. Viewed from a safe distance, say from central Africa or Tibet, it would certainly look as if this fraction had projected its own unconscious mental derangements upon nations still possessed of healthy instincts.

327   Because the things of the inner world influence us all the more powerfully for being unconscious, it is essential for anyone who intends to make progress in self-culture (and does not all culture begin with the individual?) to objectivate the effects of the anima and then try to understand what contents underlie those effects. In this way he adapts to, and is protected against, the invisible. No adaptation can result without concessions to both worlds. From a consideration of the claims of the inner and outer worlds, or rather, from the conflict between them, the possible and the necessary follows. Unfortunately our Western mind, lacking all culture in this respect, has never yet devised a concept, nor even a name, for the *union of opposites through the middle path*, that most fundamental item of inward experience, which could respectably be set against the Chinese concept of Tao. It is at once the most individual fact and the most universal, the most legitimate fulfilment of the meaning of the individual's life.

328   In the course of my exposition so far, I have kept exclusively to *masculine* psychology. The anima, being of feminine gender, is exclusively a figure that compensates the masculine consciousness. In woman the compensating figure is of a masculine character, and can therefore appropriately be termed the *animus*. If it was no easy task to describe what is meant by the anima, the difficulties become almost insuperable when we set out to describe the psychology of the animus.

329   The fact that a man naïvely ascribes his anima reactions to himself, without seeing that he really cannot identify himself with an autonomous complex, is repeated in feminine psychology, though if possible in even more marked form. This identification with an autonomous complex is the essential reason why it is so difficult to understand and describe the problem, quite apart from its inherent obscurity and strangeness. We always start with the naïve assumption that we are masters in our own house. Hence we must first accustom ourselves to the thought that, in our most intimate psychic life as well, we live in a kind of house which has doors and windows to the world, but that,

although the objects or contents of this world act upon us, they do not belong to us. For many people this hypothesis is by no means easy to conceive, just as they do not find it at all easy to understand and to accept the fact that their neighbour's psychology is not necessarily identical with their own. My reader may think that the last remark is something of an exaggeration, since in general one is aware of individual differences. But it must be remembered that our individual conscious psychology develops out of an original state of unconsciousness and therefore of non-differentiation (termed by Lévy-Bruhl *participation mystique*). Consequently, consciousness of differentiation is a relatively late achievement of mankind, and presumably but a relatively small sector of the indefinitely large field of original identity. Differentiation is the essence, the *sine qua non* of consciousness. Everything unconscious is undifferentiated, and everything that happens unconsciously proceeds on the basis of non-differentiation—that is to say, there is no determining whether it belongs or does not belong to oneself. It cannot be established *a priori* whether it concerns me, or another, or both. Nor does feeling give us any sure clues in this respect.

330   An inferior consciousness cannot *eo ipso* be ascribed to women; it is merely different from masculine consciousness. But, just as a woman is often clearly conscious of things which a man is still groping for in the dark, so there are naturally fields of experience in a man which, for woman, are still wrapped in the shadows of non-differentiation, chiefly things in which she has little interest. Personal relations are as a rule more important and interesting to her than objective facts and their interconnections. The wide fields of commerce, politics, technology, and science, the whole realm of the applied masculine mind, she relegates to the penumbra of consciousness; while, on the other hand, she develops a minute consciousness of personal relationships, the infinite nuances of which usually escape the man entirely.

331   We must therefore expect the unconscious of woman to show aspects essentially different from those found in man. If I were to attempt to put in a nutshell the difference between man and woman in this respect, i.e., what it is that characterizes the animus as opposed to the anima, I could only say this: as the anima produces *moods,* so the animus produces *opinions;* and as the

95

moods of a man issue from a shadowy background, so the opinions of a woman rest on equally unconscious prior assumptions. Animus opinions very often have the character of solid convictions that are not lightly shaken, or of principles whose validity is seemingly unassailable. If we analyse these opinions, we immediately come upon unconscious assumptions whose existence must first be inferred; that is to say, the opinions are apparently conceived *as though* such assumptions existed. But in reality the opinions are not thought out at all; they exist ready made, and they are held so positively and with so much conviction that the woman never has the shadow of a doubt about them.

332   One would be inclined to suppose that the animus, like the anima, personifies itself in a single figure. But this, as experience shows, is true only up to a point, because another factor unexpectedly makes its appearance, which brings about an essentially different situation from that existing in a man. The animus does not appear as one person, but as a plurality of persons. In H. G. Wells' novel *Christina Alberta's Father,* the heroine, in all that she does or does not do, is constantly under the surveillance of a supreme moral authority, which tells her with remorseless precision and dry matter-of-factness what she is doing and for what motives. Wells calls this authority a "Court of Conscience." This collection of condemnatory judges, a sort of College of Preceptors, corresponds to a personification of the animus. The animus is rather like an assembly of fathers or dignitaries of some kind who lay down incontestable, "rational," *ex cathedra* judgments. On closer examination these exacting judgments turn out to be largely sayings and opinions scraped together more or less unconsciously from childhood on, and compressed into a canon of average truth, justice, and reasonableness, a compendium of preconceptions which, whenever a conscious and competent judgment is lacking (as not infrequently happens), instantly obliges with an opinion. Sometimes these opinions take the form of so-called sound common sense, sometimes they appear as principles which are like a travesty of education: "People have always done it like this," or "Everybody says it is like that."

333   It goes without saying that the animus is just as often projected as the anima. The men who are particularly suited to these projections are either walking replicas of God himself, who know all about everything, or else they are misunderstood

96

word-addicts with a vast and windy vocabulary at their command, who translate common or garden reality into the terminology of the sublime. It would be insufficient to characterize the animus merely as a conservative, collective conscience; he is also a neologist who, in flagrant contradiction to his correct opinions, has an extraordinary weakness for difficult and unfamiliar words which act as a pleasant substitute for the odious task of reflection.

334   Like the anima, the animus is a jealous lover. He is an adept at putting, in place of the real man, an opinion about him, the exceedingly disputable grounds for which are never submitted to criticism. Animus opinions are invariably collective, and they override individuals and individual judgments in exactly the same way as the anima thrusts her emotional anticipations and projections between man and wife. If the woman happens to be pretty, these animus opinions have for the man something rather touching and childlike about them, which makes him adopt a benevolent, fatherly, professorial manner. But if the woman does not stir his sentimental side, and competence is expected of her rather than appealing helplessness and stupidity, then her animus opinions irritate the man to death, chiefly because they are based on nothing but opinion for opinion's sake, and "everybody has a right to his own opinions." Men can be pretty venomous here, for it is an inescapable fact that the animus always plays up the anima—and *vice versa,* of course—so that all further discussion becomes pointless.

335   In intellectual women the animus encourages a critical disputatiousness and would-be highbrowism, which, however, consists essentially in harping on some irrelevant weak point and nonsensically making it the main one. Or a perfectly lucid discussion gets tangled up in the most maddening way through the introduction of a quite different and if possible perverse point of view. Without knowing it, such women are solely intent upon exasperating the man and are, in consequence, the more completely at the mercy of the animus. "Unfortunately I am always right," one of these creatures once confessed to me.

336   However, all these traits, as familiar as they are unsavoury, are simply and solely due to the extraversion of the animus. The animus does not belong to the function of conscious relationship; his function is rather to facilitate relations with the uncon-

scious. Instead of the woman merely associating opinions with external situations—situations which she ought to think about consciously—the animus, as an associative function, should be directed inwards, where it could associate the contents of the unconscious. The technique of coming to terms with the animus is the same in principle as in the case of the anima; only here the woman must learn to criticize and hold her opinions at a distance; not in order to repress them, but, by investigating their origins, to penetrate more deeply into the background, where she will then discover the primordial images, just as the man does in his dealings with the anima. The animus is the deposit, as it were, of all woman's ancestral experiences of man—and not only that, he is also a creative and procreative being, not in the sense of masculine creativity, but in the sense that he brings forth something we might call the λόγος σπερματικός, the spermatic word. Just as a man brings forth his work as a complete creation out of his inner feminine nature, so the inner masculine side of a woman brings forth creative seeds which have the power to fertilize the feminine side of the man. This would be the *femme inspiratrice* who, if falsely cultivated, can turn into the worst kind of dogmatist and high-handed pedagogue—a regular "animus hound," as one of my women patients aptly expressed it.

337   A woman possessed by the animus is always in danger of losing her femininity, her adapted feminine persona, just as a man in like circumstances runs the risk of effeminacy. These psychic changes of sex are due entirely to the fact that a function which belongs inside has been turned outside. The reason for this perversion is clearly the failure to give adequate recognition to an inner world which stands autonomously opposed to the outer world, and makes just as serious demands on our capacity for adaptation.

338   With regard to the plurality of the animus as distinguished from what we might call the "uni-personality" of the anima, this remarkable fact seems to me to be a correlate of the conscious attitude. The conscious attitude of woman is in general far more exclusively personal than that of man. Her world is made up of fathers and mothers, brothers and sisters, husbands and children. The rest of the world consists likewise of families, who nod to each other but are, in the main, interested essentially in

themselves. The man's world is the nation, the state, business concerns, etc. His family is simply a means to an end, one of the foundations of the state, and his wife is not necessarily *the* woman for him (at any rate not as the woman means it when she says "my man"). The general means more to him than the personal; his world consists of a multitude of co-ordinated factors, whereas her world, outside her husband, terminates in a sort of cosmic mist. A passionate exclusiveness therefore attaches to the man's anima, and an indefinite variety to the woman's animus. Whereas the man has, floating before him, in clear outlines, the alluring form of a Circe or a Calypso, the animus is better expressed as a bevy of Flying Dutchmen or unknown wanderers from over the sea, never quite clearly grasped, protean, given to persistent and violent motion. These personifications appear especially in dreams, though in concrete reality they can be famous tenors, boxing champions, or great men in far-away, unknown cities.

339   These two crepuscular figures from the dark hinterland of the psyche—truly the semi-grotesque "guardians of the threshold," to use the pompous jargon of theosophy—can assume an almost inexhaustible number of shapes, enough to fill whole volumes. Their complicated transformations are as rich and strange as the world itself, as manifold as the limitless variety of their conscious correlate, the persona. They inhabit the twilight sphere, and we can just make out that the autonomous complex of anima and animus is essentially a psychological function that has usurped, or rather retained, a "personality" only because this function is itself autonomous and undeveloped. But already we can see how it is possible to break up the personifications, since by making them conscious we convert them into bridges to the unconscious. It is because we are not using them purposefully as functions that they remain personified complexes. So long as they are in this state they must be accepted as relatively independent personalities. They cannot be integrated into consciousness while their contents remain unknown. The purpose of the dialectical process is to bring these contents into the light; and only when this task has been completed, and the conscious mind has become sufficiently familiar with the unconscious processes reflected in the anima, will the anima be felt simply as a function.

340   I do not expect every reader to grasp right away what is meant by animus and anima. But I hope he will at least have gained the impression that it is not a question of anything "metaphysical," but far rather of empirical facts which could equally well be expressed in rational and abstract language. I have purposely avoided too abstract a terminology because, in matters of this kind, which hitherto have been so inaccessible to our experience, it is useless to present the reader with an intellectual formulation. It is far more to the point to give him some conception of what the actual possibilities of experience are. Nobody can really understand these things unless he has experienced them himself. I am therefore much more interested in pointing out the possible ways to such experience than in devising intellectual formulae which, for lack of experience, must necessarily remain an empty web of words. Unfortunately there are all too many who learn the words by heart and add the experiences in their heads, thereafter abandoning themselves, according to temperament, either to credulity or to criticism. We are concerned here with a new questioning, a new—and yet age-old—field of psychological experience. We shall be able to establish relatively valid theories about it only when the corresponding psychological facts are known to a sufficient number of people. The first things to be discovered are always facts, not theories. Theory-building is the outcome of discussion among many.

II

PSYCHOLOGICAL ASPECTS OF THE MOTHER ARCHETYPE

[First published as a lecture, "Die psychologischen Aspekte des Mutterarchetypus," in *Eranos-Jahrbuch 1938*. Later revised and published in *Von den Wurzeln des Bewusstseins* (Zurich, 1954). The present translation is of the latter, but it is also based partially on a translation of the 1938 version by Cary F. Baynes and Ximena de Angulo, privately issued in *Spring* (New York), 1943.—EDITORS.]

1. ON THE CONCEPT OF THE ARCHETYPE

The concept of the Great Mother belongs to the field of comparative religion and embraces widely varying types of mother-goddess. The concept itself is of no immediate concern to psychology, because the image of a Great Mother in this form is rarely encountered in practice, and then only under very special conditions. The symbol is obviously a derivative of the *mother archetype*. If we venture to investigate the background of the Great Mother image from the standpoint of psychology, then the mother archetype, as the more inclusive of the two, must form the basis of our discussion. Though lengthy discussion of the *concept* of an archetype is hardly necessary at this stage, some preliminary remarks of a general nature may not be out of place.

In former times, despite some dissenting opinion and the influence of Aristotle, it was not too difficult to understand Plato's conception of the Idea as supraordinate and pre-existent to all phenomena. "Archetype," far from being a modern term, was already in use before the time of St. Augustine, and was synonymous with "Idea" in the Platonic usage. When the *Corpus Hermeticum,* which probably dates from the third century, describes God as τὸ ἀρχέτυπον φῶς, the 'archetypal light,' it expresses the idea that he is the prototype of all light; that is to say, pre-existent and supraordinate to the phenomenon "light." Were I a philosopher, I should continue in this Platonic strain and say: Somewhere, in "a place beyond the skies," there is a prototype or primordial image of the mother that is pre-existent and supraordinate to all phenomena in which the "maternal," in the broadest sense of the term, is manifest. But I am an empiricist, not a philosopher; I cannot let myself presuppose that my peculiar temperament, my own attitude to intellectual problems, is universally valid. Apparently this is an assumption in which only the philosopher may indulge, who always takes it for granted that his own disposition and attitude are universal, and will not recognize the fact, if he can avoid it, that his "personal equation" conditions his philosophy. As an empiricist, I must point out that there is a temperament which regards ideas as real entities and not merely as *nomina*. It so happens—by the merest accident, one might say—that for the past two hundred years we have been living in an age in which it has become unpopular or even unintelligible to suppose that ideas could be anything but *nomina*. Anyone who continues to think as Plato did must pay for his anachronism by seeing the "supracelestial," i.e., metaphysical, essence of the Idea relegated to the unverifiable realm of faith and superstition, or charitably left to the poet. Once again, in the age-old controversy over universals, the nominalistic standpoint has triumphed over the realistic, and the Idea has evaporated into a mere *flatus vocis*. This change was accompanied—and, indeed, to a considerable degree caused—by the marked rise of empiricism, the advantages of which were only too obvious to the intellect. Since that time the Idea is no longer something *a priori,* but is secondary and derived. Naturally, the new nominalism promptly claimed universal validity for itself in spite of the fact that it, too, is based on a definite and limited thesis coloured by temperament. This thesis runs as follows: we accept as valid anything that comes from outside and can be verified. The ideal instance is verification by experiment. The antithesis is: we accept as valid anything that comes from inside and cannot be verified. The hopelessness of this position is obvious. Greek natural philosophy with its interest in matter, together with Aristotelian reasoning, has achieved a belated but overwhelming victory over Plato.

150   Yet every victory contains the germ of future defeat. In our own day signs foreshadowing a change of attitude are rapidly increasing. Significantly enough, it is Kant's doctrine of categories, more than anything else, that destroys in embryo every attempt to revive metaphysics in the old sense of the word, but at the same time paves the way for a rebirth of the Platonic spirit. If it be true that there can be no metaphysics transcending human reason, it is no less true that there can be no empirical knowledge that is not already caught and limited by the *a priori* structure of cognition. During the century and a half that have elapsed since the appearance of the *Critique of Pure Reason,* the conviction has gradually gained ground that thinking, under-

standing, and reasoning cannot be regarded as independent processes subject only to the eternal laws of logic, but that they are *psychic functions* co-ordinated with the personality and subordinate to it. We no longer ask, "Has this or that been seen, heard, handled, weighed, counted, thought, and found to be logical?" We ask instead, "*Who* saw, heard, or thought?" Beginning with "the personal equation" in the observation and measurement of minimal processes, this critical attitude has gone on to the creation of an empirical psychology such as no time before ours has known. Today we are convinced that in all fields of knowledge psychological premises exist which exert a decisive influence upon the choice of material, the method of investigation, the nature of the conclusions, and the formulation of hypotheses and theories. We have even come to believe that Kant's personality was a decisive conditioning factor of his *Critique of Pure Reason*. Not only our philosophers, but our own predilections in philosophy, and even what we are fond of calling our "best" truths are affected, if not dangerously undermined, by this recognition of a personal premise. All creative freedom, we cry out, is taken away from us! What? Can it be possible that a man only thinks or says or does what he himself *is*?

151   Provided that we do not again exaggerate and so fall a victim to unrestrained "psychologizing," it seems to me that the critical standpoint here defined is inescapable. It constitutes the essence, origin, and method of modern psychology. There *is* an *a priori* factor in all human activities, namely the inborn, preconscious and unconscious individual structure of the psyche. The preconscious psyche—for example, that of a new-born infant—is not an empty vessel into which, under favourable conditions, practically anything can be poured. On the contrary, it is a tremendously complicated, sharply defined individual entity which appears indeterminate to us only because we cannot see it directly. But the moment the first visible manifestations of psychic life begin to appear, one would have to be blind not to recognize their individual character, that is, the unique personality behind them. It is hardly possible to suppose that all these details come into being only at the moment in which they appear. When it is a case of morbid predispositions already present in the parents, we infer hereditary transmission through

the germ-plasm; it would not occur to us to regard epilepsy in the child of an epileptic mother as an unaccountable mutation. Again, we explain by heredity the gifts and talents which can be traced back through whole generations. We explain in the same way the reappearance of complicated instinctive actions in animals that have never set eyes on their parents and therefore could not possibly have been "taught" by them.

152   Nowadays we have to start with the hypothesis that, so far as predisposition is concerned, there is no essential difference between man and all other creatures. Like every animal, he possesses a preformed psyche which breeds true to his species and which, on closer examination, reveals distinct features traceable to family antecedents. We have not the slightest reason to suppose that there are certain human activities or functions that could be exempted from this rule. We are unable to form any idea of what those dispositions or aptitudes are which make instinctive actions in animals possible. And it is just as impossible for us to know the nature of the preconscious psychic disposition that enables a child to react in a human manner. We can only suppose that his behaviour results from patterns of functioning, which I have described as *images*. The term "image" is intended to express not only the form of the activity taking place, but the typical situation in which the activity is released.[1] These images are "primordial" images in so far as they are peculiar to whole species, and if they ever "originated" their origin must have coincided at least with the beginning of the species. They are the "human quality" of the human being, the specifically human form his activities take. This specific form is hereditary and is already present in the germ-plasm. The idea that it is not inherited but comes into being in every child anew would be just as preposterous as the primitive belief that the sun which rises in the morning is a different sun from that which set the evening before.

153   Since everything psychic is preformed, this must also be true of the individual functions, especially those which derive directly from the unconscious predisposition. The most important of these is creative fantasy. In the products of fantasy the primordial images are made visible, and it is here that the concept of the archetype finds its specific application. I do not claim to

1 Cf. my "Instinct and the Unconscious," par. 277.

have been the first to point out this fact. The honour belongs to Plato. The first investigator in the field of ethnology to draw attention to the widespread occurrence of certain "elementary ideas" was Adolf Bastian. Two later investigators, Hubert and Mauss,[2] followers of Dürkheim, speak of "categories" of the imagination. And it was no less an authority than Hermann Usener [3] who first recognized unconscious preformation under the guise of "unconscious thinking." If I have any share in these discoveries, it consists in my having shown that archetypes are not disseminated only by tradition, language, and migration, but that they can rearise spontaneously, at any time, at any place, and without any outside influence.

154   The far-reaching implications of this statement must not be overlooked. For it means that there are present in every psyche forms which are unconscious but nonetheless active—living dispositions, ideas in the Platonic sense, that preform and continually influence our thoughts and feelings and actions.

155   Again and again I encounter the mistaken notion that an archetype is determined in regard to its content, in other words that it is a kind of unconscious idea (if such an expression be admissible). It is necessary to point out once more that archetypes are not determined as regards their content, but only as regards their form and then only to a very limited degree. A primordial image is determined as to its content only when it has become conscious and is therefore filled out with the material of conscious experience. Its form, however, as I have explained elsewhere, might perhaps be compared to the axial system of a crystal, which, as it were, preforms the crystalline structure in the mother liquid, although it has no material existence of its own. This first appears according to the specific way in which the ions and molecules aggregate. The archetype in itself is empty and purely formal, nothing but a *facultas praeformandi*, a possibility of representation which is given *a priori*. The representations themselves are not inherited, only the forms, and in that respect they correspond in every way to the instincts, which are also determined in form only. The existence of the instincts can no more be proved than the existence of the archetypes, so long as they do not manifest them-

2 [Cf. the previous paper, "Concerning the Archetypes," par. 137, n. 25.—EDITORS.]
3 Usener, *Das Weihnachtsfest*, p. 3.

selves concretely. With regard to the definiteness of the form, our comparison with the crystal is illuminating inasmuch as the axial system determines only the stereometric structure but not the concrete form of the individual crystal. This may be either large or small, and it may vary endlessly by reason of the different size of its planes or by the growing together of two crystals. The only thing that remains constant is the axial system, or rather, the invariable geometric proportions underlying it. The same is true of the archetype. In principle, it can be named and has an invariable nucleus of meaning—but always only in principle, never as regards its concrete manifestation. In the same way, the specific appearance of the mother-image at any given time cannot be deduced from the mother archetype alone, but depends on innumerable other factors.

2. THE MOTHER ARCHETYPE

56 Like any other archetype, the mother archetype appears under an almost infinite variety of aspects. I mention here only some of the more characteristic. First in importance are the personal mother and grandmother, stepmother and mother-in-law; then any woman with whom a relationship exists—for example, a nurse or governess or perhaps a remote ancestress. Then there are what might be termed mothers in a figurative sense. To this category belongs the goddess, and especially the Mother of God, the Virgin, and Sophia. Mythology offers many variations of the mother archetype, as for instance the mother who reappears as the maiden in the myth of Demeter and Kore; or the mother who is also the beloved, as in the Cybele-Attis myth. Other symbols of the mother in a figurative sense appear in things representing the goal of our longing for redemption, such as Paradise, the Kingdom of God, the Heavenly Jerusalem. Many things arousing devotion or feelings of awe, as for instance the Church, university, city or country, heaven, earth, the woods, the sea or any still waters, matter even, the underworld and the moon, can be mother-symbols. The archetype is often associated with things and places standing for fertility and fruitfulness: the cornucopia, a ploughed field, a garden. It can be attached to a rock, a cave, a tree, a spring, a deep well, or to various vessels such as the baptismal font, or to vessel-shaped flowers like the rose or the lotus. Because of the protection it implies, the magic circle or mandala can be a form of mother archetype. Hollow objects such as ovens and cooking vessels are associated with the mother archetype, and, of course, the uterus, *yoni,* and anything of a like shape. Added to this list there are many animals, such as the cow, hare, and helpful animals in general.

57 All these symbols can have a positive, favourable meaning or a negative, evil meaning. An ambivalent aspect is seen in the goddesses of fate (Moira, Graeae, Norns). Evil symbols are the

witch, the dragon (or any devouring and entwining animal, such as a large fish or a serpent), the grave, the sarcophagus, deep water, death, nightmares and bogies (Empusa, Lilith, etc.). This list is not, of course, complete; it presents only the most important features of the mother archetype.

158   The qualities associated with it are maternal solicitude and sympathy; the magic authority of the female; the wisdom and spiritual exaltation that transcend reason; any helpful instinct or impulse; all that is benign, all that cherishes and sustains, that fosters growth and fertility. The place of magic transformation and rebirth, together with the underworld and its inhabitants, are presided over by the mother. On the negative side the mother archetype may connote anything secret, hidden, dark; the abyss, the world of the dead, anything that devours, seduces, and poisons, that is terrifying and inescapable like fate. All these attributes of the mother archetype have been fully described and documented in my book *Symbols of Transformation*. There I formulated the ambivalence of these attributes as "the loving and the terrible mother." Perhaps the historical example of the dual nature of the mother most familiar to us is the Virgin Mary, who is not only the Lord's mother, but also, according to the medieval allegories, his cross. In India, "the loving and terrible mother" is the paradoxical Kali. Sankhya philosophy has elaborated the mother archetype into the concept of *prakṛti* (matter) and assigned to it the three *gunas* or fundamental attributes: *sattva, rajas, tamas:* goodness, passion, and darkness.[1] These are three essential aspects of the mother: her cherishing and nourishing goodness, her orgiastic emotionality, and her Stygian depths. The special feature of the philosophical myth, which shows Prakṛti dancing before Purusha in order to remind him of "discriminating knowledge," does not belong to the mother archetype but to the archetype of the anima, which in a man's psychology invariably appears, at first, mingled with the mother-image.

159   Although the figure of the mother as it appears in folklore is more or less universal, this image changes markedly when it appears in the individual psyche. In treating patients one is at

[1] This is the etymological meaning of the three *gunas*. See Weckerling, *Ananda-raya-makhi: Das Glück des Lebens*, pp. 21 ff., and Garbe, *Die Samkhya Philosophie*, pp. 272ff. [Cf. also Zimmer, *Philosophies of India*, index, s.v.—EDITORS.]

first impressed, and indeed arrested, by the apparent significance of the personal mother. This figure of the personal mother
looms so large in all personalistic psychologies that, as we know,
they never got beyond it, even in theory, to other important
aetiological factors. My own view differs from that of other
medico-psychological theories principally in that I attribute to
the personal mother only a limited aetiological significance.
That is to say, all those influences which the literature describes
as being exerted on the children do not come from the mother
herself, but rather from the archetype projected upon her, which
gives her a mythological background and invests her with authority and numinosity.[2] The aetiological and traumatic effects
produced by the mother must be divided into two groups: (1)
those corresponding to traits of character or attitudes actually
present in the mother, and (2) those referring to traits which
the mother only seems to possess, the reality being composed of
more or less fantastic (i.e., archetypal) projections on the part of
the child. Freud himself had already seen that the real aetiology
of neuroses does not lie in traumatic effects, as he at first suspected, but in a peculiar development of infantile fantasy. This
is not to deny that such a development can be traced back to
disturbing influences emanating from the mother. I myself make
it a rule to look first for the cause of infantile neuroses in the
mother, as I know from experience that a child is much more
likely to develop normally than neurotically, and that in the
great majority of cases definite causes of disturbances can be
found in the parents, especially in the mother. The contents of
the child's abnormal fantasies can be referred to the personal
mother only in part, since they often contain clear and unmis-
takable allusions which could not possibly have reference to
human beings. This is especially true where definitely mythological products are concerned, as is frequently the case in
infantile phobias where the mother may appear as a wild beast,
a witch, a spectre, an ogre, a hermaphrodite, and so on. It must
be borne in mind, however, that such fantasies are not always of
unmistakably mythological origin, and even if they are, they
may not always be rooted in the unconscious archetype but may
have been occasioned by fairytales or accidental remarks. A

2 American psychology can supply us with any amount of examples. A blistering
but instructive lampoon on this subject is Philip Wylie's *Generation of Vipers*.

thorough investigation is therefore indicated in each case. For practical reasons, such an investigation cannot be made so readily with children as with adults, who almost invariably transfer their fantasies to the physician during treatment—or, to be more precise, the fantasies are projected upon him automatically.

160   When that happens, nothing is gained by brushing them aside as ridiculous, for archetypes are among the inalienable assets of every psyche. They form the "treasure in the realm of shadowy thoughts" of which Kant spoke, and of which we have ample evidence in the countless treasure motifs of mythology. An archetype is in no sense just an annoying prejudice; it becomes so only when it is in the wrong place. In themselves, archetypal images are among the highest values of the human psyche; they have peopled the heavens of all races from time immemorial. To discard them as valueless would be a distinct loss. Our task is not, therefore, to deny the archetype, but to dissolve the projections, in order to restore their contents to the individual who has involuntarily lost them by projecting them outside himself.

3. THE MOTHER-COMPLEX

61 The mother archetype forms the foundation of the so-called mother-complex. It is an open question whether a mother-complex can develop without the mother having taken part in its formation as a demonstrable causal factor. My own experience leads me to believe that the mother always plays an active part in the origin of the disturbance, especially in infantile neuroses or in neuroses whose aetiology undoubtedly dates back to early childhood. In any event, the child's instincts are disturbed, and this constellates archetypes which, in their turn, produce fantasies that come between the child and its mother as an alien and often frightening element. Thus, if the children of an over-anxious mother regularly dream that she is a terrifying animal or a witch, these experiences point to a split in the child's psyche that predisposes it to a neurosis.

I. THE MOTHER-COMPLEX OF THE SON

62 The effects of the mother-complex differ according to whether it appears in a son or a daughter. Typical effects on the son are homosexuality and Don Juanism, and sometimes also impotence.[1] In homosexuality, the son's entire heterosexuality is tied to the mother in an unconscious form; in Don Juanism, he unconsciously seeks his mother in every woman he meets. The effects of a mother-complex on the son may be seen in the ideology of the Cybele and Attis type: self-castration, madness, and early death. Because of the difference in sex, a son's mother-complex does not appear in pure form. This is the reason why in every masculine mother-complex, side by side with the mother archetype, a significant role is played by the image of the man's sexual counterpart, the anima. The mother is the first feminine being with whom the man-to-be comes in contact, and

1 But the father-complex also plays a considerable part here.

she cannot help playing, overtly or covertly, consciously or unconsciously, upon the son's masculinity, just as the son in his turn grows increasingly aware of his mother's femininity, or unconsciously responds to it by instinct. In the case of the son, therefore, the simple relationships of identity or of resistance and differentiation are continually cut across by erotic attraction or repulsion, which complicates matters very considerably. I do not mean to say that for this reason the mother-complex of a son ought to be regarded as more serious than that of a daughter. The investigation of these complex psychic phenomena is still in the pioneer stage. Comparisons will not become feasible until we have some statistics at our disposal, and of these, so far, there is no sign.

163   Only in the daughter is the mother-complex clear and uncomplicated. Here we have to do either with an overdevelopment of feminine instincts indirectly caused by the mother, or with a weakening of them to the point of complete extinction. In the first case, the preponderance of instinct makes the daughter unconscious of her own personality; in the latter, the instincts are projected upon the mother. For the present we must content ourselves with the statement that in the daughter a mother-complex either unduly stimulates or else inhibits the feminine instinct, and that in the son it injures the masculine instinct through an unnatural sexualization.

164   Since a "mother-complex" is a concept borrowed from psychopathology, it is always associated with the idea of injury and illness. But if we take the concept out of its narrow psychopathological setting and give it a wider connotation, we can see that it has positive effects as well. Thus a man with a mother-complex may have a finely differentiated Eros [2] instead of, or in addition to, homosexuality. (Something of this sort is suggested by Plato in his *Symposium*.) This gives him a great capacity for friendship, which often creates ties of astonishing tenderness between men and may even rescue friendship between the sexes from the limbo of the impossible. He may have good taste and an aesthetic sense which are fostered by the presence of a feminine streak. Then he may be supremely gifted as a teacher because of his almost feminine insight and tact. He is likely to have a feeling for history, and to be conservative in the best

2 [Cf. *Two Essays on Analytical Psychology*, pars. 16ff.—EDITORS.]

sense and cherish the values of the past. Often he is endowed with a wealth of religious feelings, which help to bring the *ecclesia spiritualis* into reality; and a spiritual receptivity which makes him responsive to revelation.

⁶5   In the same way, what in its negative aspect is Don Juanism can appear positively as bold and resolute manliness; ambitious striving after the highest goals; opposition to all stupidity, narrow-mindedness, injustice, and laziness; willingness to make sacrifices for what is regarded as right, sometimes bordering on heroism; perseverance, inflexibility and toughness of will; a curiosity that does not shrink even from the riddles of the universe; and finally, a revolutionary spirit which strives to put a new face upon the world.

66   All these possibilities are reflected in the mythological motifs enumerated earlier as different aspects of the mother archetype. As I have already dealt with the mother-complex of the son, including the anima complication, elsewhere, and my present theme is the archetype of the mother, in the following discussion I shall relegate masculine psychology to the background.

II. THE MOTHER-COMPLEX OF THE DAUGHTER [3]

67   (a) *Hypertrophy of the Maternal Element.*—We have noted that in the daughter the mother-complex leads either to a hypertrophy of the feminine side or to its atrophy. The exaggeration of the feminine side means an intensification of all female instincts, above all the maternal instinct. The negative aspect is seen in the woman whose only goal is childbirth. To her the husband is obviously of secondary importance; he is first and foremost the instrument of procreation, and she regards him merely as an object to be looked after, along with children, poor relations, cats, dogs, and household furniture. Even her own

---

[3] In the present section I propose to present a series of different "types" of mother-complex; in formulating them, I am drawing on my own therapeutic experiences. "Types" are not individual cases, neither are they freely invented schemata into which all individual cases have to be fitted. "Types" are ideal instances, or pictures of the average run of experience, with which no single individual can be identified. People whose experience is confined to books or psychological laboratories can form no proper idea of the cumulative experience of a practising psychologist.

personality is of secondary importance; she often remains entirely unconscious of it, for her life is lived in and through others, in more or less complete identification with all the objects of her care. First she gives birth to the children, and from then on she clings to them, for without them she has no existence whatsoever. Like Demeter, she compels the gods by her stubborn persistence to grant her the right of possession over her daughter. Her Eros develops exclusively as a maternal relationship while remaining unconscious as a personal one. An unconscious Eros always expresses itself as will to power.[4] Women of this type, though continually "living for others," are, as a matter of fact, unable to make any real sacrifice. Driven by ruthless will to power and a fanatical insistence on their own maternal rights, they often succeed in annihilating not only their own personality but also the personal lives of their children. The less conscious such a mother is of her own personality, the greater and the more violent is her unconscious will to power. For many such women Baubo rather than Demeter would be the appropriate symbol. The mind is not cultivated for its own sake but usually remains in its original condition, altogether primitive, unrelated, and ruthless, but also as true, and sometimes as profound, as Nature herself.[5] She herself does not know this and is therefore unable to appreciate the wittiness of her mind or to marvel philosophically at its profundity; like as not she will immediately forget what she has said.

168   (b) *Overdevelopment of Eros.*—It by no means follows that the complex induced in a daughter by such a mother must necessarily result in hypertrophy of the maternal instinct. Quite the contrary, this instinct may be wiped out altogether. As a substitute, an overdeveloped Eros results, and this almost invariably leads to an unconscious incestuous relationship with the father.[6] The intensified Eros places an abnormal emphasis on the personality of others. Jealousy of the mother and the desire to outdo her become the leitmotifs of subsequent undertakings, which

4 This statement is based on the repeated experience that, where love is lacking, power fills the vacuum.

5 In my English seminars [privately distributed] I have called this the "natural mind."

6 Here the initiative comes from the daughter. In other cases the father's psychology is responsible; his projection of the anima arouses an incestuous fixation in the daughter.

are often disastrous. A woman of this type loves romantic and sensational episodes for their own sake, and is interested in married men, less for themselves than for the fact that they are married and so give her an opportunity to wreck a marriage, that being the whole point of her manoeuvre. Once the goal is attained, her interest evaporates for lack of any maternal instinct, and then it will be someone else's turn.[7] This type is noted for its remarkable unconsciousness. Such women really seem to be utterly blind to what they are doing,[8] which is anything but advantageous either for themselves or for their victims. I need hardly point out that for men with a passive Eros this type offers an excellent hook for anima projections.

69   (c) *Identity with the Mother.*—If a mother-complex in a woman does not produce an overdeveloped Eros, it leads to identification with the mother and to paralysis of the daughter's feminine initiative. A complete projection of her personality on to the mother then takes place, owing to the fact that she is unconscious both of her maternal instinct and of her Eros. Everything which reminds her of motherhood, responsibility, personal relationships, and erotic demands arouses feelings of inferiority and compels her to run away—to her mother, naturally, who lives to perfection everything that seems unattainable to her daughter. As a sort of superwoman (admired involuntarily by the daughter), the mother lives out for her beforehand all that the girl might have lived for herself. She is content to cling to her mother in selfless devotion, while at the same time unconsciously striving, almost against her will, to tyrannize over her, naturally under the mask of complete loyalty and devotion. The daughter leads a shadow-existence, often visibly sucked dry by her mother, and she prolongs her mother's life by a sort of continuous blood transfusion. These bloodless maidens are by no means immune to marriage. On the contrary, despite their shadowiness and passivity, they command a high price on the marriage market. First, they are so empty that a man is free to impute to them anything he fancies. In addition, they are so unconscious that the unconscious puts out countless invisible

7 Herein lies the difference between this type of complex and the feminine father-complex related to it, where the "father" is mothered and coddled.
8 This does not mean that they are unconscious of the *facts*. It is only their *meaning* that escapes them.

feelers, veritable octopus-tentacles, that suck up all masculine projections; and this pleases men enormously. All that feminine indefiniteness is the longed-for counterpart of male decisiveness and single-mindedness, which can be satisfactorily achieved only if a man can get rid of everything doubtful, ambiguous, vague, and muddled by projecting it upon some charming example of feminine innocence.[9] Because of the woman's characteristic passivity, and the feelings of inferiority which make her continually play the injured innocent, the man finds himself cast in an attractive role: he has the privilege of putting up with the familiar feminine foibles with real superiority, and yet with forbearance, like a true knight. (Fortunately, he remains ignorant of the fact that these deficiencies consist largely of his own projections.) The girl's notorious helplessness is a special attraction. She is so much an appendage of her mother that she can only flutter confusedly when a man approaches. She just doesn't know a thing. She is so inexperienced, so terribly in need of help, that even the gentlest swain becomes a daring abductor who brutally robs a loving mother of her daughter. Such a marvellous opportunity to pass himself off as a gay Lothario does not occur every day and therefore acts as a strong incentive. This was how Pluto abducted Persephone from the inconsolable Demeter. But, by a decree of the gods, he had to surrender his wife every year to his mother-in-law for the summer season. (The attentive reader will note that such legends do not come about by chance!)

170   (d) *Resistance to the Mother.*—These three extreme types are linked together by many intermediate stages, of which I shall mention only one important example. In the particular intermediate type I have in mind, the problem is less an over-development or an inhibition of the feminine instincts than an overwhelming resistance to maternal supremacy, often to the exclusion of all else. It is the supreme example of the negative mother-complex. The motto of this type is: Anything, so long as it is not like Mother! On one hand we have a fascination which never reaches the point of identification; on the other, an intensification of Eros which exhausts itself in jealous resist-

[9] This type of woman has an oddly disarming effect on her husband, but only until he discovers that the person he has married and who shares his nuptial bed is his mother-in-law.

ance. This kind of daughter knows what she does *not* want, but is usually completely at sea as to what she would choose as her own fate. All her instincts are concentrated on the mother in the negative form of resistance and are therefore of no use to her in building her own life. Should she get as far as marrying, either the marriage will be used for the sole purpose of escaping from her mother, or else a diabolical fate will present her with a husband who shares all the essential traits of her mother's character. All instinctive processes meet with unexpected difficulties; either sexuality does not function properly, or the children are unwanted, or maternal duties seem unbearable, or the demands of marital life are responded to with impatience and irritation. This is quite natural, since none of it has anything to do with the realities of life when stubborn resistance to the power of the mother in every form has come to be life's dominating aim. In such cases one can often see the attributes of the mother archetype demonstrated in every detail. For example, the mother as representative of the family (or clan) causes either violent resistances or complete indifference to anything that comes under the head of family, community, society, convention, and the like. Resistance to the mother as *uterus* often manifests itself in menstrual disturbances, failure of conception, abhorrence of pregnancy, hemorrhages and excessive vomiting during pregnancy, miscarriages, and so on. The mother as *materia,* 'matter,' may be at the back of these women's impatience with objects, their clumsy handling of tools and crockery and bad taste in clothes.

171   Again, resistance to the mother can sometimes result in a spontaneous development of intellect for the purpose of creating a sphere of interest in which the mother has no place. This development springs from the daughter's own needs and not at all for the sake of a man whom she would like to impress or dazzle by a semblance of intellectual comradeship. Its real purpose is to break the mother's power by intellectual criticism and superior knowledge, so as to enumerate to her all her stupidities, mistakes in logic, and educational shortcomings. Intellectual development is often accompanied by the emergence of masculine traits in general.

4. POSITIVE ASPECTS OF THE MOTHER-COMPLEX

I. THE MOTHER

72 The positive aspect of the first type of complex, namely the overdevelopment of the maternal instinct, is identical with that well-known image of the mother which has been glorified in all ages and all tongues. This is the mother-love which is one of the most moving and unforgettable memories of our lives, the mysterious root of all growth and change; the love that means homecoming, shelter, and the long silence from which everything begins and in which everything ends. Intimately known and yet strange like Nature, lovingly tender and yet cruel like fate, joyous and untiring giver of life—*mater dolorosa* and mute implacable portal that closes upon the dead. Mother is mother-love, *my* experience and *my* secret. Why risk saying too much, too much that is false and inadequate and beside the point, about that human being who was our mother, the accidental carrier of that great experience which includes herself and myself and all mankind, and indeed the whole of created nature, the experience of life whose children we are? The attempt to say these things has always been made, and probably always will be; but a sensitive person cannot in all fairness load that enormous burden of meaning, responsibility, duty, heaven and hell, on to the shoulders of one frail and fallible human being—so deserving of love, indulgence, understanding, and forgiveness—who was our mother. He knows that the mother carries for us that inborn image of the *mater natura* and *mater spiritualis,* of the totality of life of which we are a small and helpless art. Nor should we hesitate for one moment to relieve the human mother of this appalling burden, for our own sakes as well as hers. It is just this massive weight of meaning that ties us to the mother and chains her to her child, to the physical and mental

detriment of both. A mother-complex is not got rid of by blindly reducing the mother to human proportions. Besides that we run the risk of dissolving the experience "Mother" into atoms, thus destroying something supremely valuable and throwing away the golden key which a good fairy laid in our cradle. That is why mankind has always instinctively added the pre-existent divine pair to the personal parents—the "god"-father and "god"-mother of the newborn child—so that, from sheer unconsciousness or shortsighted rationalism, he should never forget himself so far as to invest his own parents with divinity.

173   The archetype is really far less a scientific problem than an urgent question of psychic hygiene. Even if all proofs of the existence of archetypes were lacking, and all the clever people in the world succeeded in convincing us that such a thing could not possibly exist, we would have to invent them forthwith in order to keep our highest and most important values from disappearing into the unconscious. For when these fall into the unconscious the whole elemental force of the original experience is lost. What then appears in its place is fixation on the mother-imago; and when this has been sufficiently rationalized and "corrected," we are tied fast to human reason and condemned from then on to believe exclusively in what is rational. That is a virtue and an advantage on the one hand, but on the other a limitation and impoverishment, for it brings us nearer to the bleakness of doctrinairism and "enlightenment." This Déesse Raison emits a deceptive light which illuminates only what we know already, but spreads a darkness over all those things which it would be most needful for us to know and become conscious of. The more independent "reason" pretends to be, the more it turns into sheer intellectuality which puts doctrine in the place of reality and shows us man not as he is but how it wants him to be.

174   Whether he understands them or not, man must remain conscious of the world of the archetypes, because in it he is still a part of Nature and is connected with his own roots. A view of the world or a social order that cuts him off from the primordial images of life not only is no culture at all but, in increasing degree, is a prison or a stable. If the primordial images remain conscious in some form or other, the energy that belongs to

them can flow freely into man. But when it is no longer possible to maintain contact with them, then the tremendous sum of energy stored up in these images, which is also the source of the fascination underlying the infantile parental complex, falls back into the unconscious. The unconscious then becomes charged with a force that acts as an irresistible *vis a tergo* to whatever view or idea or tendency our intellect may choose to dangle enticingly before our desiring eyes. In this way man is delivered over to his conscious side, and reason becomes the arbiter of right and wrong, of good and evil. I am far from wishing to belittle the divine gift of reason, man's highest faculty. But in the role of absolute tyrant it has no meaning—no more than light would have in a world where its counterpart, darkness, was absent. Man would do well to heed the wise counsel of the mother and obey the inexorable law of nature which sets limits to every being. He ought never to forget that the world exists only because opposing forces are held in equilibrium. So, too, the rational is counterbalanced by the irrational, and what is planned and purposed by what *is*.

175   This excursion into the realm of generalities was unavoidable, because the mother is the first world of the child and the last world of the adult. We are all wrapped as her children in the mantle of this great Isis. But let us now return to the different types of feminine mother-complex. It may seem strange that I am devoting so much more time to the mother-complex in woman than to its counterpart in man. The reason for this has already been mentioned: in a man, the mother-complex is never "pure," it is always mixed with the anima archetype, and the consequence is that a man's statements about the mother are always emotionally prejudiced in the sense of showing "animosity." Only in women is it possible to examine the effects of the mother archetype without admixture of animosity, and even this has prospects of success only when no compensating animus has developed.

II. THE OVERDEVELOPED EROS

176   I drew a very unfavourable picture of this type as we encounter it in the field of psychopathology. But this type, uninviting

as it appears, also has positive aspects which society could ill afford to do without. Indeed, behind what is possibly the worst effect of this attitude, the unscrupulous wrecking of marriages, we can see an extremely significant and purposeful arrangement of nature. This type often develops in reaction to a mother who is wholly a thrall of nature, purely instinctive and therefore all-devouring. Such a mother is an anachronism, a throw-back to a primitive state of matriarchy where the man leads an insipid existence as a mere procreator and serf of the soil. The reactive intensification of the daughter's Eros is aimed at some man who ought to be rescued from the preponderance of the female-maternal element in his life. A woman of this type instinctively intervenes when provoked by the unconsciousness of the marriage partner. She will disturb that comfortable ease so dangerous to the personality of a man but frequently regarded by him as marital faithfulness. This complacency leads to blank unconsciousness of his own personality and to those supposedly ideal marriages where he is nothing but Dad and she is nothing but Mom, and they even call each other that. This is a slippery path that can easily degrade marriage to the level of a mere breeding-pen.

177   A woman of this type directs the burning ray of her Eros upon a man whose life is stifled by maternal solicitude, and by doing so she arouses a moral conflict. Yet without this there can be no consciousness of personality. "But why on earth," you may ask, "should it be necessary for man to achieve, by hook or by crook, a higher level of consciousness?" This is truly the crucial question, and I do not find the answer easy. Instead of a real answer I can only make a confession of faith: I believe that, after thousands and millions of years, someone had to realize that this wonderful world of mountains and oceans, suns and moons, galaxies and nebulae, plants and animals, *exists*. From a low hill in the Athi plains of East Africa I once watched the vast herds of wild animals grazing in soundless stillness, as they had done from time immemorial, touched only by the breath of a primeval world. I felt then as if I were the first man, the first creature, to know that all this *is*. The entire world round me was still in its primeval state; it did not know that it *was*. And then, in that one moment in which I came to know, the world sprang into being; without that moment it would never have

been. All Nature seeks this goal and finds it fulfilled in man, but only in the most highly developed and most fully conscious man. Every advance, even the smallest, along this path of conscious realization adds that much to the world.

178   There is no consciousness without discrimination of opposites. This is the paternal principle, the Logos, which eternally struggles to extricate itself from the primal warmth and primal darkness of the maternal womb; in a word, from unconsciousness. Divine curiosity yearns to be born and does not shrink from conflict, suffering, or sin. Unconsciousness is the primal sin, evil itself, for the Logos. Therefore its first creative act of liberation is matricide, and the spirit that dared all heights and all depths must, as Synesius says, suffer the divine punishment, enchainment on the rocks of the Caucasus. Nothing can exist without its opposite; the two were one in the beginning and will be one again in the end. Consciousness can only exist through continual recognition of the unconscious, just as everything that lives must pass through many deaths.

179   The stirring up of conflict is a Luciferian virtue in the true sense of the word. Conflict engenders fire, the fire of affects and emotions, and like every other fire it has two aspects, that of combustion and that of creating light. On the one hand, emotion is the alchemical fire whose warmth brings everything into existence and whose heat burns all superfluities to ashes (*omnes superfluitates comburit*). But on the other hand, emotion is the moment when steel meets flint and a spark is struck forth, for emotion is the chief source of consciousness. There is no change from darkness to light or from inertia to movement without emotion.

180   The woman whose fate it is to be a disturbing element is not solely destructive, except in pathological cases. Normally the disturber is herself caught in the disturbance; the worker of change is herself changed, and the glare of the fire she ignites both illuminates and enlightens all the victims of the entanglement. What seemed a senseless upheaval becomes a process of purification:

> So that all that is vain
> Might dwindle and wane.[1]

1 *Faust*, Part II, Act 5.

181   If a woman of this type remains unconscious of the meaning of her function, if she does not know that she is

> Part of that power which would
> Ever work evil but engenders good,[2]

she will herself perish by the sword she brings. But consciousness transforms her into a deliverer and redeemer.

III. THE "NOTHING-BUT" DAUGHTER

182   The woman of the third type, who is so identified with the mother that her own instincts are paralysed through projection, need not on that account remain a hopeless nonentity forever. On the contrary, if she is at all normal, there is a good chance of the empty vessel being filled by a potent anima projection. Indeed, the fate of such a woman depends on this eventuality; she can never find herself at all, not even approximately, without a man's help; she has to be literally abducted or stolen from her mother. Moreover, she must play the role mapped out for her for a long time and with great effort, until she actually comes to loathe it. In this way she may perhaps discover who she really is. Such women may become devoted and self-sacrificing wives of husbands whose whole existence turns on their identification with a profession or a great talent, but who, for the rest, are unconscious and remain so. Since they are nothing but masks themselves, the wife, too, must be able to play the accompanying part with a semblance of naturalness. But these women sometimes have valuable gifts which remained undeveloped only because they were entirely unconscious of their own personality. They may project the gift or talent upon a husband who lacks it himself, and then we have the spectacle of a totally insignificant man who seemed to have no chance whatsoever suddenly soaring as if on a magic carpet to the highest summits of achievement. *Cherchez la femme,* and you have the secret of his success. These women remind me—if I may be forgiven the impolite comparison—of hefty great bitches who turn tail before the smallest cur simply because he is a terrible male and it never occurs to them to bite him.

2 Ibid., Part I, Act 1.

183   Finally, it should be remarked that *emptiness* is a great feminine secret. It is something absolutely alien to man; the chasm, the unplumbed depths, the *yin*. The pitifulness of this vacuous nonentity goes to his heart (I speak here as a man), and one is tempted to say that this constitutes the whole "mystery" of woman. Such a female is fate itself. A man may say what he likes about it; be for it or against it, or both at once; in the end he falls, absurdly happy, into this pit, or, if he doesn't, he has missed and bungled his only chance of making a man of himself. In the first case one cannot disprove his foolish good luck to him, and in the second one cannot make his misfortune seem plausible. "The Mothers, the Mothers, how eerily it sounds!"[3] With this sigh, which seals the capitulation of the male as he approaches the realm of the Mothers, we will turn to the fourth type.

IV. THE NEGATIVE MOTHER-COMPLEX

184   As a pathological phenomenon this type is an unpleasant, exacting, and anything but satisfactory partner for her husband, since she rebels in every fibre of her being against everything that springs from natural soil. However, there is no reason why increasing experience of life should not teach her a thing or two, so that for a start she gives up fighting the mother in the personal and restricted sense. But even at her best she will remain hostile to all that is dark, unclear, and ambiguous, and will cultivate and emphasize everything certain and clear and reasonable. Excelling her more feminine sister in her objectivity and coolness of judgment, she may become the friend, sister, and competent adviser of her husband. Her own masculine aspirations make it possible for her to have a human understanding of the individuality of her husband quite transcending the realm of the erotic. The woman with this type of mother-complex probably has the best chance of all to make her marriage an outstanding success during the second half of life. But this is true only if she succeeds in overcoming the hell of "nothing but femininity," the chaos of the maternal womb, which is her greatest danger because of her negative complex. As we know, a com-

3 Ibid., Part II, Act 1.

plex can be really overcome only if it is lived out to the full. In other words, if we are to develop further we have to draw to us and drink down to the very dregs what, because of our complexes, we have held at a distance.

185   This type started out in the world with averted face, like Lot's wife looking back on Sodom and Gomorrah. And all the while the world and life pass by her like a dream—an annoying source of illusions, disappointments, and irritations, all of which are due solely to the fact that she cannot bring herself to look straight ahead for once. Because of her merely unconscious, reactive attitude toward reality, her life actually becomes dominated by what she fought hardest against—the exclusively maternal feminine aspect. But if she should later turn her face, she will see the world for the first time, so to speak, in the light of maturity, and see it embellished with all the colours and enchanting wonders of youth, and sometimes even of childhood. It is a vision that brings knowledge and discovery of truth, the indispensable prerequisite for consciousness. A part of life was lost, but the meaning of life has been salvaged for her.

186   The woman who fights against her father still has the possibility of leading an instinctive, feminine existence, because she rejects only what is alien to her. But when she fights against the mother she may, at the risk of injury to her instincts, attain to greater consciousness, because in repudiating the mother she repudiates all that is obscure, instinctive, ambiguous, and unconscious in her own nature. Thanks to her lucidity, objectivity, and masculinity, a woman of this type is frequently found in important positions in which her tardily discovered maternal quality, guided by a cool intelligence, exerts a most beneficial influence. This rare combination of womanliness and masculine understanding proves valuable in the realm of intimate relationships as well as in practical matters. As the spiritual guide and adviser of a man, such a woman, unknown to the world, may play a highly influential part. Owing to her qualities, the masculine mind finds this type easier to understand than women with other forms of mother-complex, and for this reason men often favour her with the projection of positive mother-complexes. The excessively feminine woman terrifies men who have a mother-complex characterized by great sensitivity. But this woman is not frightening to a man, because she builds bridges

for the masculine mind over which he can safely guide his feelings to the opposite shore. Her clarity of understanding inspires him with confidence, a factor not to be underrated and one that is absent from the relationship between a man and a woman much more often than one might think. The man's Eros does not lead upward only but downward into that uncanny dark world of Hecate and Kali, which is a horror to any intellectual man. The understanding possessed by this type of woman will be a guiding star to him in the darkness and seemingly unending mazes of life.

5. CONCLUSION

187   From what has been said it should be clear that in the last analysis all the statements of mythology on this subject as well as the observed effects of the mother-complex, when stripped of their confusing detail, point to the unconscious as their place of origin. How else could it have occurred to man to divide the cosmos, on the analogy of day and night, summer and winter, into a bright day-world and a dark night-world peopled with fabulous monsters, unless he had the prototype of such a division in himself, in the polarity between the conscious and the invisible and unknowable unconscious? Primitive man's perception of objects is conditioned only partly by the objective behaviour of the things themselves, whereas a much greater part is often played by intrapsychic facts which are not related to the external objects except by way of projection.[1] This is due to the simple fact that the primitive has not yet experienced that ascetic discipline of mind known to us as the critique of knowledge. To him the world is a more or less fluid phenomenon within the stream of his own fantasy, where subject and object are undifferentiated and in a state of mutual interpenetration. "All that is outside, also is inside," we could say with Goethe. But this "inside," which modern rationalism is so eager to derive from "outside," has an *a priori* structure of its own that antedates all conscious experience. It is quite impossible to conceive how "experience" in the widest sense, or, for that matter, anything psychic, could originate exclusively in the outside world. The psyche is part of the inmost mystery of life, and it has its own peculiar structure and form like every other organism. Whether this psychic structure and its elements, the archetypes, ever "originated" at all is a metaphysical question and therefore unanswerable. The structure is something given, the precondition that is found to be present in every case. And this is the *mother*, the matrix—the form into which all experience is

1 [Cf. above, "Archetypes of the Collective Unconscious," par. 7.—EDITORS.]

poured. The *father,* on the other hand, represents the *dynamism* of the archetype, for the archetype consists of both—form and energy.

188   The carrier of the archetype is in the first place the personal mother, because the child lives at first in complete participation with her, in a state of unconscious identity. She is the psychic as well as the physical precondition of the child. With the awakening of ego-consciousness the participation gradually weakens, and consciousness begins to enter into opposition to the unconscious, its own precondition. This leads to differentiation of the ego from the mother, whose personal peculiarities gradually become more distinct. All the fabulous and mysterious qualities attaching to her image begin to fall away and are transferred to the person closest to her, for instance the grandmother. As the mother of the mother, she is "greater" than the latter; she is in truth the "grand" or "Great Mother." Not infrequently she assumes the attributes of wisdom as well as those of a witch. For the further the archetype recedes from consciousness and the clearer the latter becomes, the more distinctly does the archetype assume mythological features. The transition from mother to grandmother means that the archetype is elevated to a higher rank. This is clearly demonstrated in a notion held by the Bataks. The funeral sacrifice in honour of a dead father is modest, consisting of ordinary food. But if the son has a son of his own, then the father has become a grandfather and has consequently attained a more dignified status in the Beyond, and very important offerings are made to him.[2]

189   As the distance between conscious and unconscious increases, the grandmother's more exalted rank transforms her into a "Great Mother," and it frequently happens that the opposites contained in this image split apart. We then get a good fairy and a wicked fairy, or a benevolent goddess and one who is malevolent and dangerous. In Western antiquity and especially in Eastern cultures the opposites often remain united in the same figure, though this paradox does not disturb the primitive mind in the least. The legends about the gods are as full of contradictions as are their moral characters. In the West, the paradoxical behaviour and moral ambivalence of the gods scandalized people even in antiquity and gave rise to criticism that led

[2] Warnecke, *Die Religion der Batak.*

finally to a devaluation of the Olympians on the one hand and to their philosophical interpretation on the other. The clearest expression of this is the Christian reformation of the Jewish concept of the Deity: the morally ambiguous Yahweh became an exclusively good God, while everything evil was united in the devil. It seems as if the development of the feeling function in Western man forced a choice on him which led to the moral splitting of the divinity into two halves. In the East the predominantly intuitive intellectual attitude left no room for feeling values, and the gods—Kali is a case in point—could retain their original paradoxical morality undisturbed. Thus Kali is representative of the East and the Madonna of the West. The latter has entirely lost the shadow that still distantly followed her in the allegories of the Middle Ages. It was relegated to the hell of popular imagination, where it now leads an insignificant existence as the devil's grandmother.[3] Thanks to the development of feeling-values, the splendour of the "light" god has been enhanced beyond measure, but the darkness supposedly represented by the devil has localized itself in man. This strange development was precipitated chiefly by the fact that Christianity, terrified of Manichaean dualism, strove to preserve its monotheism by main force. But since the reality of darkness and evil could not be denied, there was no alternative but to make man responsible for it. Even the devil was largely, if not entirely, abolished, with the result that this metaphysical figure, who at one time was an integral part of the Deity, was introjected into man, who thereupon became the real carrier of the *mysterium iniquitatis:* "omne bonum a Deo, omne malum ab homine." In recent times this development has suffered a diabolical reverse, and the wolf in sheep's clothing now goes about whispering in our ear that evil is really nothing but a misunderstanding of good and an effective instrument of progress. We think that the world of darkness has thus been abolished for good and all, and nobody realizes what a poisoning this is of man's soul. In this way he turns himself into the devil, for the devil is half of the archetype whose irresistible power makes even unbelievers ejaculate "Oh God!" on every suitable and unsuitable occasion. If one can possibly avoid it, one ought never to identify with an archetype, for, as psychopathology

3 [A familiar figure of speech in German.—EDITORS.]

and certain contemporary events show, the consequences are terrifying.

190　　Western man has sunk to such a low level spiritually that he even has to deny the apotheosis of untamed and untameable psychic power—the divinity itself—so that, after swallowing evil, he may possess himself of the good as well. If you read Nietzsche's *Zarathustra* with attention and psychological understanding, you will see that he has described with rare consistency and with the passion of a truly religious person the psychology of the "Superman" for whom God is dead, and who is himself burst asunder because he tried to imprison the divine paradox within the narrow framework of the mortal man. Goethe has wisely said: "What terror then shall seize the Superman!"—and was rewarded with a supercilious smile from the Philistines. His glorification of the Mother who is great enough to include in herself both the Queen of Heaven and Maria Aegyptiaca is supreme wisdom and profoundly significant for anyone willing to reflect upon it. But what can one expect in an age when the official spokesmen of Christianity publicly announce their inability to understand the foundations of religious experience! I extract the following sentence from an article by a Protestant theologian: "We understand ourselves—whether naturalistically or idealistically—to be *homogeneous creatures who are not so peculiarly divided that alien forces can intervene in our inner life,* as the New Testament supposes." [4] (Italics mine.) The author is evidently unacquainted with the fact that science demonstrated the lability and dissociability of consciousness more than half a century ago and proved it by experiment. Our conscious intentions are continually disturbed and thwarted, to a greater or lesser degree, by unconscious intrusions whose causes are at first strange to us. The psyche is far from being a homogeneous unit—on the contrary, it is a boiling cauldron of contradictory impulses, inhibitions, and affects, and for many people the conflict between them is so insupportable that they even wish for the deliverance preached by theologians. Deliverance from what? Obviously, from a highly questionable psychic state. The unity of consciousness or of the so-called personality is not a reality at all but a desideratum. I still have a vivid memory of a certain philosopher who also raved about this unity and

4 Buri, "Theologie und Philosophie," p. 117. [Quoting Rudolf Bultmann.—EDs.]

used to consult me about his neurosis: he was obsessed by the idea that he was suffering from cancer. I do not know how many specialists he had consulted already, and how many X-ray pictures he had had made. They all assured him that he had no cancer. He himself told me: "I know I have no cancer, but I still could have one." Who is responsible for this "imaginary" idea? He certainly did not make it himself; it was forced on him by an "alien" power. There is little to choose between this state and that of the man possessed in the New Testament. Now whether you believe in a demon of the air or in a factor in the unconscious that plays diabolical tricks on you is all one to me. The fact that man's imagined unity is menaced by alien powers remains the same in either case. Theologians would do better to take account for once of these psychological facts than to go on "demythologizing" them with rationalistic explanations that are a hundred years behind the times.

*

91   I have tried in the foregoing to give a survey of the psychic phenomena that may be attributed to the predominance of the mother-image. Although I have not always drawn attention to them, my reader will presumably have had no difficulty in recognizing those features which characterize the Great Mother mythologically, even when they appear under the guise of personalistic psychology. When we ask patients who are particularly influenced by the mother-image to express in words or pictures what "Mother" means to them—be it positive or negative— we invariably get symbolical figures which must be regarded as direct analogies of the mythological mother-image. These analogies take us into a field that still requires a great deal more work of elucidation. At any rate, I personally do not feel able to say anything definitive about it. If, nevertheless, I venture to offer a few suggestions, they should be regarded as altogether provisional and tentative.

92   Above all, I should like to point out that the mother-image in a man's psychology is entirely different in character from a woman's. For a woman, the mother typifies her own conscious life as conditioned by her sex. But for a man the mother typifies something alien, which he has yet to experience and which is filled with the imagery latent in the unconscious. For this

reason, if for no other, the mother-image of a man is essentially different from a woman's. The mother has from the outset a decidedly symbolical significance for a man, which probably accounts for his strong tendency to idealize her. Idealization is a hidden apotropaism; one idealizes whenever there is a secret fear to be exorcized. What is feared is the unconscious and its magical influence.[5]

193   Whereas for a man the mother is *ipso facto* symbolical, for a woman she becomes a symbol only in the course of her psychological development. Experience reveals the striking fact that the Urania type of mother-image predominates in masculine psychology, whereas in a woman the chthonic type, or Earth Mother, is the most frequent. During the manifest phase of the archetype an almost complete identification takes place. A woman can identify directly with the Earth Mother, but a man cannot (except in psychotic cases). As mythology shows, one of the peculiarities of the Great Mother is that she frequently appears paired with her male counterpart. Accordingly the man identifies with the son-lover on whom the grace of Sophia has descended, with a *puer aeternus* or a *filius sapientiae*. But the companion of the chthonic mother is the exact opposite: an ithyphallic Hermes (the Egyptian Bes) or a lingam. In India this symbol is of the highest spiritual significance, and in the West Hermes is one of the most contradictory figures of Hellenistic syncretism, which was the source of extremely important spiritual developments in Western civilization. He is also the god of revelation, and in the unofficial nature philosophy of the early Middle Ages he is nothing less than the world-creating Nous itself. This mystery has perhaps found its finest expression in the words of the *Tabula smaragdina:* "omne superius sicut inferius" (as it is above, so it is below).

194   It is a psychological fact that as soon as we touch on these identifications we enter the realm of the syzygies, the paired opposites, where the One is never separated from the Other, its antithesis. It is a field of personal experience which leads directly to the experience of individuation, the attainment of the self. A vast number of symbols for this process could be mustered from the medieval literature of the West and even more

[5] Obviously a daughter can idealize her mother too, but for this special circumstances are needed, whereas in a man idealization is almost the normal thing.

from the storehouses of Oriental wisdom, but in this matter words and ideas count for little. Indeed, they may become dangerous bypaths and false trails. In this still very obscure field of psychological experience, where we are in direct contact, so to speak, with the archetype, its psychic power is felt in full force. This realm is so entirely one of immediate experience that it cannot be captured by any formula, but can only be hinted at to one who already knows. He will need no explanations to understand what was the tension of opposites expressed by Apuleius in his magnificent prayer to the Queen of Heaven, when he associates "heavenly Venus" with "Proserpina, who strikest terror with midnight ululations": [6] it was the terrifying paradox of the primordial mother-image.

*

195   When, in 1938, I originally wrote this paper, I naturally did not know that twelve years later the Christian version of the mother archetype would be elevated to the rank of a dogmatic truth. The Christian "Queen of Heaven" has, obviously, shed all her Olympian qualities except for her brightness, goodness, and eternality; and even her human body, the thing most prone to gross material corruption, has put on an ethereal incorruptibility. The richly varied allegories of the Mother of God have nevertheless retained some connection with her pagan prefigurations in Isis (Io) and Semele. Not only are Isis and the Horus-child iconological exemplars, but the ascension of Semele, the originally mortal mother of Dionysus, likewise anticipates the Assumption of the Blessed Virgin. Further, this son of Semele is a dying and resurgent god and the youngest of the Olympians. Semele herself seems to have been an earth-goddess, just as the Virgin Mary is the earth from which Christ was born. This being so, the question naturally arises for the psychologist: what has become of the characteristic relation of the mother-image to the earth, darkness, the abysmal side of the bodily man with his animal passions and instinctual nature, and to "matter" in general? The declaration of the dogma comes at a time when the achievements of science and technology, combined with a rationalistic and materialistic view of the world, threaten

[6] "Nocturnis ululatibus horrenda Proserpina." Cf. *Symbols of Transformation*, par. 148.

the spiritual and psychic heritage of man with instant annihilation. Humanity is arming itself, in dread and fascinated horror, for a stupendous crime. Circumstances might easily arise when the hydrogen bomb would have to be used and the unthinkably frightful deed became unavoidable in legitimate self-defence. In striking contrast to this disastrous turn of events, the Mother of God is now enthroned in heaven; indeed, her Assumption has actually been interpreted as a deliberate counterstroke to the materialistic doctrinairism that provoked the chthonic powers into revolt. Just as Christ's appearance in his own day created a real devil and adversary of God out of what was originally a son of God dwelling in heaven, so now, conversely, a heavenly figure has split off from her original chthonic realm and taken up a counter-position to the titanic forces of the earth and the underworld that have been unleashed. In the same way that the Mother of God was divested of all the essential qualities of materiality, matter became completely de-souled, and this at a time when physics is pushing forward to insights which, if they do not exactly "de-materialize" matter, at least endue it with properties of its own and make its relation to the psyche a problem that can no longer be shelved. For just as the tremendous advancement of science led at first to a premature dethronement of mind and to an equally ill-considered deification of matter, so it is this same urge for scientific knowledge that is now attempting to bridge the huge gulf that has opened out between the two *Weltanschauungen*. The psychologist inclines to see in the dogma of the Assumption a symbol which, in a sense, anticipates this whole development. For him the relationship to the earth and to matter is one of the inalienable qualities of the mother archetype. So that when a figure that is conditioned by this archetype is represented as having been taken up into heaven, the realm of the spirit, this indicates a union of earth and heaven, or of matter and spirit. The approach of natural science will almost certainly be from the other direction: it will see in matter itself the equivalent of spirit, but this "spirit" will appear divested of all, or at any rate most, of its known qualities, just as earthly matter was stripped of its specific characteristics when it staged its entry into heaven. Nevertheless, the way will gradually be cleared for a union of the two principles.

96   Understood concretely, the Assumption is the absolute opposite of materialism. Taken in this sense, it is a counterstroke that
does nothing to diminish the tension between the opposites, but
drives it to extremes.

97   Understood symbolically, however, the Assumption of the
body is a recognition and acknowledgment of matter, which in
the last resort was identified with evil only because of an over-
whelmingly "pneumatic" tendency in man. In themselves, spirit
and matter are neutral, or rather, "utriusque capax"—that is,
capable of what man calls good or evil. Although as names they
are exceedingly relative, underlying them are very real opposites
that are part of the energic structure of the physical and of the
psychic world, and without them no existence of any kind could
be established. There is no position without its negation. In
spite or just because of their extreme opposition, neither can exist
without the other. It is exactly as formulated in classical Chinese
philosophy: *yang* (the light, warm, dry, masculine principle)
contains within it the seed of *yin* (the dark, cold, moist, feminine
principle), and vice versa. Matter therefore would contain the
seed of spirit and spirit the seed of matter. The long-known
"synchronistic" phenomena that have now been statistically
confirmed by Rhine's experiments [7] point, to all appearances,
in this direction. The "psychization" of matter puts the absolute
immateriality of spirit in question, since this would then have
to be accorded a kind of substantiality. The dogma of the Assumption, proclaimed in an age suffering from the greatest
political schism history has ever known, is a compensating
symptom that reflects the strivings of science for a uniform
world-picture. In a certain sense, both developments were antici-
pated by alchemy in the *hieros gamos* of opposites, but only in
symbolic form. Nevertheless, the symbol has the great advantage
of being able to unite heterogeneous or even incommensurable
factors in a *single* image. With the decline of alchemy the
symbolical unity of spirit and matter fell apart, with the result
that modern man finds himself uprooted and alienated in a
de-souled world.

98   The alchemist saw the union of opposites under the symbol
of the tree, and it is therefore not surprising that the unconscious of present-day man, who no longer feels at home in his

7 Cf. my "Synchronicity: An Acausal Connecting Principle."

world and can base his existence neither on the past that is no more nor on the future that is yet to be, should hark back to the symbol of the cosmic tree rooted in this world and growing up to heaven—the tree that is also man. In the history of symbols this tree is described as the way of life itself, a growing into that which eternally is and does not change; which springs from the union of opposites and, by its eternal presence, also makes that union possible. It seems as if it were only through an experience of symbolic reality that man, vainly seeking his own "existence" and making a philosophy out of it, can find his way back to a world in which he is no longer a stranger.

III

THE PSYCHOLOGICAL ASPECTS
OF THE KORE

THE PSYCHOLOGICAL ASPECTS OF THE KORE

306 Not only is the figure of Demeter and the Kore in its three-fold aspect as maiden, mother, and Hecate not unknown to the psychology of the unconscious, it is even something of a practical problem. The "Kore" has her psychological counterpart in those archetypes which I have called the *self* or *supraordinate personality* on the one hand, and the *anima* on the other. In order to explain these figures, with which I cannot assume all readers to be familiar, I must begin with some remarks of a general nature.

307 The psychologist has to contend with the same difficulties as the mythologist when an exact definition or clear and concise information is demanded of him. The picture is concrete, clear, and subject to no misunderstandings only when it is seen in its habitual context. In this form it tells us everything it contains. But as soon as one tries to abstract the "real essence" of the picture, the whole thing becomes cloudy and indistinct. In order to understand its living function, we must let it remain an organic thing in all its complexity and not try to examine the anatomy of its corpse in the manner of the scientist, or the archaeology of its ruins in the manner of the historian. Naturally this is not to deny the justification of such methods when applied in their proper place.

308 In view of the enormous complexity of psychic phenomena, a purely phenomenological point of view is, and will be for a long time, the only possible one and the only one with any prospect of success. "Whence" things come and "what" they are, these, particularly in the field of psychology, are questions which are apt to call forth untimely attempts at explanation. Such speculations are moreover based far more on unconscious philosophical premises than on the nature of the phenomena themselves. Psychic phenomena occasioned by unconscious processes are so rich and so multifarious that I prefer to *describe* my findings and observations and, where possible, to classify them—

that is, to arrange them under certain definite types. That is the method of natural science, and it is applied wherever we have to do with multifarious and still unorganized material. One may question the utility or the appropriateness of the categories or types used in the arrangement, but not the correctness of the method itself.

309   Since for years I have been observing and investigating the products of the unconscious in the widest sense of the word, namely dreams, fantasies, visions, and delusions of the insane, I have not been able to avoid recognizing certain regularities, that is, *types*. There are types of *situations* and types of *figures* that repeat themselves frequently and have a corresponding meaning. I therefore employ the term "motif" to designate these repetitions. Thus there are not only typical dreams but typical motifs in the dreams. These may, as we have said, be situations or figures. Among the latter there are human figures that can be arranged under a series of archetypes, the chief of them being, according to my suggestion,[1] the *shadow*, the *wise old man*, the *child* (including the child hero), the *mother* ("Primordial Mother" and "Earth Mother") as a supraordinate personality ("daemonic" because supraordinate), and her counterpart the *maiden*, and lastly the *anima* in man and the *animus* in woman.

310   The above types are far from exhausting all the statistical regularities in this respect. The figure of the Kore that interests us here belongs, when observed in a man, to the *anima* type; and when observed in a woman to the type of *supraordinate personality*. It is an essential characteristic of psychic figures that they are duplex or at least capable of duplication; at all events they are bipolar and oscillate between their positive and negative meanings. Thus the "supraordinate" personality can appear in a despicable and distorted form, like for instance Mephistopheles, who is really more positive as a personality than the vapid and unthinking careerist Faust. Another negative figure

[1] To the best of my knowledge, no other suggestions have been made so far. Critics have contented themselves with asserting that no such archetypes exist. Certainly they do not exist, any more than a botanical system exists in nature! But will anyone deny the existence of natural plant-families on that account? Or will anyone deny the occurrence and continual repetition of certain morphological and functional similarities? It is much the same thing in principle with the typical figures of the unconscious. They are forms existing *a priori*, or biological norms of psychic activity.

is the Tom Thumb or Tom Dumb of the folktales. The figure corresponding to the Kore in a woman is generally a double one, i.e., a mother and a maiden, which is to say that she appears now as the one, now as the other. From this I would conclude, for a start, that in the formation of the Demeter-Kore myth the feminine influence so far outweighed the masculine that the latter had practically no significance. The man's role in the Demeter myth is really only that of seducer or conqueror.

11   As a matter of practical observation, the Kore often appears in woman as an *unknown young girl,* not infrequently as Gretchen or the unmarried mother.[2] Another frequent modulation is the *dancer,* who is often formed by borrowings from classical knowledge, in which case the "maiden" appears as the *corybant, maenad,* or *nymph.* An occasional variant is the nixie or water-sprite, who betrays her superhuman nature by her fishtail. Sometimes the Kore- and mother-figures slither down altogether to the animal kingdom, the favourite representatives then being the *cat* or the *snake* or the *bear,* or else some black monster of the underworld like the crocodile, or other salamander-like, saurian creatures.[3] The maiden's helplessness exposes her to all sorts of *dangers,* for instance of being devoured by reptiles or ritually slaughtered like a beast of sacrifice. Often there are bloody, cruel, and even obscene *orgies* to which the innocent child falls victim. Sometimes it is a true *nekyia,* a descent into Hades and a quest for the "treasure hard to attain," occasionally connected with orgiastic sexual rites or offerings of menstrual blood to the moon. Oddly enough, the various tortures and obscenities are carried out by an "Earth Mother." There are *drinkings of blood* and *bathings in blood,*[4] also cruci-

2 The "personalistic" approach interprets such dreams as "wish-fulfilments." To many, this kind of interpretation seems the only possible one. These dreams, however, occur in the most varied circumstances, even in circumstances when the wish-fulfilment theory becomes entirely forced or arbitrary. The investigation of motifs in the field of dreams therefore seems to me the more cautious and the more appropriate procedure.

3 The double vision of a salamander, of which Benvenuto Cellini tells in his autobiography, would be an anima-projection caused by the music his father was playing.

4 One of my patients, whose principal difficulty was a negative mother-complex, developed a series of fantasies on a primitive mother-figure, an Indian woman,

fixions. The maiden who crops up in case histories differs not inconsiderably from the vaguely flower-like Kore in that the modern figure is more sharply delineated and not nearly so "unconscious," as the following examples will show.

312   The figures corresponding to Demeter and Hecate are supraordinate, not to say over-life-size "Mothers" ranging from the Pietà type to the Baubo type. The unconscious, which acts as a counterbalance to woman's conventional innocuousness, proves to be highly inventive in this latter respect. I can recall only very few cases where Demeter's own noble figure in its pure form breaks through as an image rising spontaneously from the unconscious. I remember a case, in fact, where a maiden-goddess appears clad all in purest white, but carrying a black monkey in her arms. The Earth Mother is always chthonic and is occasionally related to the moon, either through the blood-sacrifice already mentioned, or through a child-sacrifice, or else because she is adorned with a sickle moon.[5] In pictorial or plastic representations the Mother is dark deepening to *black*, or *red* (these being her principal colours), and with a primitive or animal expression of face; in form she not infrequently resembles the

---

who instructed her on the nature of woman in general. In these pronouncements a special paragraph is devoted to blood, running as follows: "A woman's life is close to the *blood*. Every month she is reminded of this, and birth is indeed a bloody business, destructive and creative. A woman is only *permitted* to give birth, but the new life is not *her* creation. In her heart of hearts she knows this and rejoices in the grace that has fallen to her. She is a little mother, not the *Great Mother*. But her little pattern is like the great pattern. If she understands this she is blessed by nature, because she has submitted in the right way and can thus partake of the nourishment of the Great Mother. . . ."

[5] Often the moon is simply "there," as for instance in a fantasy of the chthonic mother in the shape of the "Woman of the Bees" (Josephine D. Bacon, *In the Border Country*, pp. 14ff.): "The path led to a tiny hut of the same colour as the *four great trees* that stood about it. Its door hung wide open, and in the middle of it, on a low stool, there sat an old woman wrapped in a long cloak, looking kindly at her. . . ." The hut was filled with the steady *humming of bees*. In the corner of the hut there was a deep cold *spring*, in which "a white moon and little stars" were reflected. The old woman exhorted the heroine to remember the duties of a woman's life. In Tantric yoga an "indistinct hum of swarms of love-mad bees" proceeds from the slumbering Shakti (*Shat-Chakra Nirupana*, in Avalon, *The Serpent Power*, p. 29). Cf. infra, the dancer who dissolves into a *swarm of bees*. Bees are also, as an allegory, connected with Mary, as the text for the consecration of the Easter candle shows. See Duchesne, *Christian Worship: Its Origin and Evolution*, p. 253.

neolithic ideal of the "Venus" of Brassempouy or that of Willendorf, or again the sleeper of Hal Saflieni.[6] Now and then I have come across *multiple breasts,* arranged like those of a sow. The Earth Mother plays an important part in the woman's unconscious, for all her manifestations are described as "powerful." This shows that in such cases the Earth Mother element in the conscious mind is abnormally weak and requires strengthening.

313   In view of all this it is, I admit, hardly understandable why such figures should be reckoned as belonging to the type of "supraordinate personality." In a scientific investigation, however, one has to disregard moral or aesthetic prejudices and let the facts speak for themselves. The *maiden* is often described as not altogether human in the usual sense; she is either of unknown or peculiar origin, or she looks strange or undergoes strange experiences, from which one is forced to infer the maiden's extraordinary, myth-like nature. Equally and still more strikingly, the Earth Mother is a divine being—in the classical sense. Moreover, she does not by any means always appear in the guise of Baubo, but, for instance, more like Queen Venus in the *Hypnerotomachia Poliphili,* though she is invariably heavy with destiny. The often unaesthetic forms of the Earth Mother are in keeping with a prejudice of the modern feminine unconscious; this prejudice was lacking in antiquity. The underworld nature of Hecate, who is closely connected with Demeter, and Persephone's fate both point nevertheless to the dark side of the human psyche, though not to the same extent as the modern material.

314   The "supraordinate personality" is the total man, i.e., man as he really is, not as he appears to himself. To this wholeness the unconscious psyche also belongs, which has its requirements and needs just as consciousness has. I do not want to interpret the unconscious personalistically and assert, for instance, that fantasy-images like those described above are the "wish-fulfilments" due to repression. These images were as such never conscious and consequently could never have been repressed. I understand the unconscious rather as an *impersonal* psyche common to all men, even though it expresses itself through a

6 [See Neumann, *The Great Mother,* Pls. 1a, 3. This entire work elucidates the present study.—EDITORS.]

147

personal consciousness. When anyone breathes, his breathing is not a phenomenon to be interpreted personally. The mythological images belong to the structure of the unconscious and are an impersonal possession; in fact, the great majority of men are far more *possessed by* them than possessing them. Images like those described above give rise under certain conditions to corresponding disturbances and symptoms, and it is then the task of medical therapy to find out whether and how and to what extent these impulses can be integrated with the conscious personality, or whether they are a secondary phenomenon which some defective orientation of consciousness has brought out of its normal potential state into actuality. Both possibilities exist in practice.

315   I usually describe the supraordinate personality as the "self," thus making a sharp distinction between the ego, which, as is well known, extends only as far as the conscious mind, and the *whole* of the personality, which includes the unconscious as well as the conscious component. The ego is thus related to the self as part to whole. To that extent the self is supraordinate. Moreover, the self is felt empirically not as subject but as object, and this by reason of its unconscious component, which can only come to consciousness indirectly, by way of projection. Because of its unconscious component the self is so far removed from the conscious mind that it can only be partially expressed by human figures; the other part of it has to be expressed by objective, abstract symbols. The human figures are father and son, mother and daughter, king and queen, god and goddess. Theriomorphic symbols are the dragon, snake, elephant, lion, bear, and other powerful animals, or again the spider, crab, butterfly, beetle, worm, etc. Plant symbols are generally flowers (lotus and rose). These lead on to geometrical figures like the circle, the sphere, the square, the quaternity, the clock, the firmament, and so on.[7] The indefinite extent of the unconscious component makes a comprehensive description of the human personality impossible. Accordingly, the unconscious supplements the picture with living figures ranging from the animal to the divine, as the two extremes outside man, and rounds out the animal extreme, through the addition of

[7] *Psychology and Alchemy*, Part II.

vegetable and inorganic abstractions, into a microcosm. These addenda have a high frequency in anthropomorphic divinities, where they appear as "attributes."

16   Demeter and Kore, mother and daughter, extend the feminine consciousness both upwards and downwards. They add an "older and younger," "stronger and weaker" dimension to it and widen out the narrowly limited conscious mind bound in space and time, giving it intimations of a greater and more comprehensive personality which has a share in the eternal course of things. We can hardly suppose that myth and mystery were invented for any conscious purpose; it seems much more likely that they were the involuntary revelation of a psychic, but unconscious, pre-condition. The psyche pre-existent to consciousness (e.g., in the child) participates in the maternal psyche on the one hand, while on the other it reaches across to the daughter psyche. We could therefore say that every mother contains her daughter in herself and every daughter her mother, and that every woman extends backwards into her mother and forwards into her daughter. This participation and intermingling give rise to that peculiar uncertainty as regards *time:* a woman lives earlier as a mother, later as a daughter. The conscious experience of these ties produces the feeling that her life is spread out over generations—the first step towards the immediate experience and conviction of being outside time, which brings with it a feeling of *immortality.* The individual's life is elevated into a type, indeed it becomes the archetype of woman's fate in general. This leads to a restoration or *apocatastasis* of the lives of her ancestors, who now, through the bridge of the momentary individual, pass down into the generations of the future. An experience of this kind gives the individual a place and a meaning in the life of the generations, so that all unnecessary obstacles are cleared out of the way of the life-stream that is to flow through her. At the same time the individual is rescued from her isolation and restored to wholeness. All ritual preoccupation with archetypes ultimately has this aim and this result.

317   It is immediately clear to the psychologist what cathartic and at the same rejuvenating effects must flow from the Demeter cult into the feminine psyche, and what a lack of psychic hygiene

characterizes our culture, which no longer knows the kind of wholesome experience afforded by Eleusinian emotions.

318   I take full account of the fact that not only the psychologically minded layman but the professional psychologist and psychiatrist as well, and even the psychotherapist, do not possess an adequate knowledge of their patients' archetypal material, in so far as they have not specially investigated this aspect of the phenomenology of the unconscious. For it is precisely in the field of psychiatric and psychotherapeutic observation that we frequently meet with cases characterized by a rich crop of archetypal symbols.[8] Since the necessary historical knowledge is lacking to the physician observing them, he is not in a position to perceive the parallelism between his observations and the findings of anthropology and the humane sciences in general. Conversely, an expert in mythology and comparative religion is as a rule no psychiatrist and consequently does not know that his mythologems are still fresh and living—for instance, in dreams and visions—in the hidden recesses of our most personal life, which we would on no account deliver up to scientific dissection. The archetypal material is therefore the great unknown, and it requires special study and preparation even to collect such material.

319   It does not seem to me superfluous to give a number of examples from my case histories which bring out the occurrence of archetypal images in dreams or fantasies. Time and again with my public I come across the difficulty that they imagine illustration by "a few examples" to be the simplest thing in the world. In actual fact it is almost impossible, with a few words and one or two images torn out of their context, to demonstrate anything. This only works when dealing with an expert. What Perseus has to do with the Gorgon's head would never occur to anyone who did not know the myth. So it is with the individual images: they need a context, and the context is not only a myth but an individual anamnesis. Such contexts, however, are of enormous extent. Anything like a complete series of images would require for its proper presentation a book of about two hundred pages. My own investigation of the Miller fantasies

---

[8] I would refer to the thesis of my pupil Jan Nelken, "Analytische Beobachtungen über Phantasien eines Schizophrenen," as also to my own analysis of a series of fantasies in *Symbols of Transformation*.

gives some idea of this.[9] It is therefore with the greatest hesitation that I make the attempt to illustrate from case-histories. The material I shall use comes partly from normal, partly from slightly neurotic, persons. It is part dream, part vision, or dream mixed with vision. These "visions" are far from being hallucinations or ecstatic states; they are spontaneous, visual images of fantasy or so-called *active imagination*. The latter is a method (devised by myself) of introspection for observing the stream of interior images. One concentrates one's attention on some impressive but unintelligible dream-image, or on a spontaneous visual impression, and observes the changes taking place in it. Meanwhile, of course, all criticism must be suspended and the happenings observed and noted with absolute objectivity. Obviously, too, the objection that the whole thing is "arbitrary" or "thought up" must be set aside, since it springs from the anxiety of an ego-consciousness which brooks no master besides itself in its own house. In other words, it is the inhibition exerted by the conscious mind on the unconscious.

20 Under these conditions, long and often very dramatic series of fantasies ensue. The advantage of this method is that it brings a mass of unconscious material to light. Drawing, painting, and modelling can be used to the same end. Once a visual series has become dramatic, it can easily pass over into the auditive or linguistic sphere and give rise to dialogues and the like. With slightly pathological individuals, and particularly in the not infrequent cases of latent schizophrenia, the method may, in certain circumstances, prove to be rather dangerous and therefore requires medical control. It is based on a deliberate weakening of the conscious mind and its inhibiting effect, which either limits or suppresses the unconscious. The aim of the method is naturally therapeutic in the first place, while in the second it also furnishes rich empirical material. Some of our examples are taken from this. They differ from dreams only by reason of their better form, which comes from the fact that the contents were perceived not by a dreaming but by a waking consciousness. The examples are from women in middle life.

9 Cf. *Symbols of Transformation*. H. G. Baynes' book, *The Mythology of the Soul*, runs to 939 pages and endeavours to do justice to the material provided by only two cases.

1. Case X (spontaneous visual impressions, in chronological order)

321   i. *"I saw a white bird with outstretched wings. It alighted on the figure of a woman, clad in blue, who sat there like an* antique statue. *The bird perched on her hand, and in it she held a grain of wheat. The bird took it in its beak and flew into the sky again."*

322   For this X painted a picture: a blue-clad, archaically simple "Mother"-figure on a white marble base. Her maternity is emphasized by the large breasts.

323   ii. *A bull lifts a child up from the ground and carries it to the antique statue of a woman. A naked young girl with a wreath of flowers in her hair appears, riding on a white bull. She takes the child and throws it into the air like a ball and catches it again. The white bull carries them both to a temple. The girl lays the child on the ground, and so on (initiation follows).*

324   In this picture the *maiden* appears, rather in the form of Europa. (Here a certain school knowledge is being made use of.) Her nakedness and the wreath of flowers point to Dionysian abandonment. The game of ball with the child is the motif of some secret rite which always has to do with "child-sacrifice." (Cf. the accusations of ritual murder levelled by the pagans against the Christians and by the Christians against the Jews and Gnostics; also the Phoenician child-sacrifices, rumours about the Black Mass, etc., and "the ball-game in church.") [10]

325   iii. *"I saw a golden* pig *on a pedestal. Beast-like beings danced round it in a circle. We made haste to dig a hole in the ground. I reached in and found water. Then a man appeared in a golden carriage. He jumped into the hole and began swaying back and forth, as if dancing. . . . I swayed in rhythm with him. Then he suddenly leaped out of the hole, raped me, and got me with child."*

326   X is identical with the young girl, who often appears as a *youth,* too. This youth is an animus-figure, the embodiment of the masculine element in a woman. Youth and young girl together form a syzygy or *coniunctio* which symbolizes the essence

[10] [Cf. infra, "On the Psychology of the Trickster-Figure."—EDITORS.]

of wholeness (as also does the Platonic hermaphrodite, who later became the symbol of perfected wholeness in alchemical philosophy). X evidently dances with the rest, hence *"we* made haste." The parallel with the motifs stressed by Kerényi seems to me remarkable.

327   iv. *"I saw a beautiful youth with golden cymbals, dancing and leaping in joy and abandonment. . . . Finally he fell to the ground and buried his face in the flowers. Then he sank into the lap of a very old mother. After a time he got up and jumped into the water, where he sported like a* dolphin. *. . . I saw that his hair was golden. Now we were leaping together, hand in hand. So we came to a gorge. . . ."* In leaping the gorge the youth falls into the chasm. X is left alone and comes to a river where a white sea-horse is waiting for her with a golden boat.

328   In this scene X is the youth; therefore he disappears later, leaving her the sole heroine of the story. She is the child of the "very old mother," and is also the dolphin, the youth lost in the gorge, and the bride evidently expected by Poseidon. The peculiar overlapping and displacement of motifs in all this individual material is about the same as in the mythological variants. X found the youth in the lap of the mother so impressive that she painted a picture of it. The figure is the same as in item i; only, instead of the grain of wheat in her hand, there is the body of the youth lying completely exhausted in the lap of the gigantic mother.

329   v. *There now follows a sacrifice of sheep, during which a game of ball is likewise played with the sacrificial animal. The participants* smear themselves with the sacrificial blood, *and afterwards bathe in the pulsing gore.* X is thereupon transformed into a plant.

330   vi. *After that X comes to a* den of snakes, *and the snakes wind all round her.*

331   vii. *In a den of snakes beneath the sea there is a* divine woman, *asleep.* (She is shown in the picture as much larger than the others.) *She is wearing a blood-red garment that covers only the lower half of her body. She has a dark skin, full red lips, and seems to be of great physical strength. She kisses X, who is obviously in the role of the young girl, and hands her as a present to the many men who are standing by, etc.*

332   This chthonic goddess is the typical Earth Mother as she appears in so many modern fantasies.

333   viii. *As X emerged from the depths and saw the light again, she experienced a kind of illumination: white flames played about her head as she walked through waving* fields of grain.

334   With this picture the Mother-episode ended. Although there is not the slightest trace of any known myth being repeated, the motifs and the connections between them are all familiar to us from mythology. These images present themselves spontaneously and are based on no conscious knowledge whatever. I have applied the method of active imagination to myself over a long time and have observed numerous symbols and symbolic associations which in many cases I was only able to verify years afterwards in texts of whose existence I was totally ignorant. It is the same with dreams. Some years ago I dreamed for example that: *I was climbing slowly and toilsomely up a mountain. When I had reached, as I imagined, the top, I found that I was standing on the edge of a plateau. The crest that represented the real top of the mountain only rose far off in the distance. Night was coming on, and I saw, on the dark slope opposite, a brook flowing down with a metallic shimmer, and two paths leading upwards, one to the left, the other to the right, winding like serpents. On the crest, to the right, there was a hotel. Down below, the brook ran to the left with a bridge leading across.*

335   Not long afterwards I discovered the following "allegory" in an obscure alchemical treatise. In his *Speculativae philosophiae* [11] the Frankfurt physician Gerard Dorn, who lived in the second half of the sixteenth century, describes the "Mundi peregrinatio, quam erroris viam appellamus" (Tour of the world, which we call the way of error) on the one hand and the "Via veritatis" on the other. Of the first way the author says:

The human race, whose nature it is to resist God, does not cease to ask how it may, by its own efforts, escape the pitfalls which it has laid for itself. But it does not ask help from Him on whom alone depends every gift of mercy. Hence it has come about that men have built for themselves a great Workshop on the left-hand side of the road . . . presided over by Industry. After this has been attained, they turn aside from Industry and bend their steps towards the

[11] *Theatrum chemicum,* I (1602), pp. 286ff.

second region of the world, making their crossing *on the bridge of infirmity.* . . . But because the good God desires to draw them back, He allows their infirmities to rule over them; then, seeking as before a remedy in themselves [industry!], they flock *to the great Hospital likewise built on the left,* presided over by Medicine. Here there is a great multitude of apothecaries, surgeons, and physicians, [etc.].[12]

336 Of the "way of truth," which is the "right" way, our author says: ". . . you will come to the camp of Wisdom and on being received there, you will be refreshed with food far more powerful than before." Even the brook is there: ". . . a stream of living water flowing with such wonderful artifice from the mountain peak. (From the Fountain of Wisdom the waters gush forth.)" [13]

337 An important difference, compared with my dream, is that here, apart from the situation of the hotel being reversed, the river of Wisdom is on the right and not, as in my dream, in the middle of the picture.

338 It is evident that in my dream we are not dealing with any known "myth" but with a group of ideas which might easily have been regarded as "individual," i.e., unique. A thorough analysis, however, could show without difficulty that it is an archetypal image such as can be reproduced over and over again in any age and any place. But I must admit that the archetypal nature of the dream-image only became clear to me when I read Dorn. These and similar incidents I have observed repeatedly not only in myself but in my patients. But, as this

12 "Humanum genus, cui Deo resistere iam innatum est, non desistit media quaerere, quibus proprio conatu laqueos evadat, quos sibimet posuit, ab eo non petens auxilium, a quo solo dependet omnis misericordiae munus. Hinc factum est, ut in sinistram viae partem officinam sibi maximam exstruxerint . . . huic domui praeest industria, etc. Quod postquam adepti fuerint, ab industria recedentes *in secundam mundi regionem* tendunt: *per infirmitatis pontem* facientes transitum. . . . At quia bonus Deus retrahere vellet, infirmitates in ipsis dominari permittit, tum rursus ut prius remedium [industria!] a se quaerentes, *ad xenodochium etiam a sinistris constructum* et permaximum confluunt, cui medicina praeest. Ibi pharmacopolarum, chirurgorum et physicorum ingens est copia." (p. 288.)

13 ". . . pervenietis ad Sophiae castra, quibus excepti, longe vehementiori quam antea cibo reficiemini. . . . viventis aquae fluvius tam admirando fluens artificio de montis apice. (De Sophiae fonte scaturiunt aquae!)" [Slightly modified by Professor Jung. Cf. Dorn, pp. 279–80.—EDITORS.]

example shows, it needs special attention if such parallels are not to be missed.

339   The antique Mother-image is not exhausted with the figure of Demeter. It also expresses itself in Cybele-Artemis. The next case points in this direction.

2. Case Y (dreams)

340   i. *"I am wandering over a great mountain; the way is lonely, wild, and difficult. A woman comes down from the sky to accompany and help me. She is all bright with light hair and shining eyes. Now and then she vanishes. After going on for some time alone I notice that I have left my stick somewhere, and must turn back to fetch it. To do this I have to pass a terrible monster, an enormous bear. When I came this way the first time I had to pass it, but then the sky-woman protected me. Just as I am passing the beast and he is about to come at me, she stands beside me again, and at her look the bear lies down quietly and lets us pass. Then the sky-woman vanishes."*

341   Here we have a maternally protective goddess related to bears, a kind of Diana or the Gallo-Roman Dea Artio. The sky-woman is the positive, the bear the negative aspect of the "supraordinate personality," which extends the conscious human being upwards into the celestial and downwards into the animal regions.

342   ii. *"We go through a door into a tower-like room, where we climb a long flight of steps. On one of the topmost steps I read an inscription: 'Vis ut sis.' The steps end in a temple situated on the crest of a wooded mountain, and there is no other approach. It is the shrine of* Ursanna, *the bear-goddess and Mother of God in one. The temple is of red stone. Bloody sacrifices are offered there. Animals are standing about the altar. In order to enter the temple precincts one has to be transformed into an animal—a beast of the forest. The temple has the form of a cross with equal arms and a circular space in the middle, which is not roofed, so that one can look straight up at the sky and the constellation of the Bear. On the altar in the middle of the open space there stands the moon-bowl, from which smoke or vapour continually rises. There is also a huge image of the goddess, but it cannot be seen clearly. The worshippers, who*

*have been changed into animals and to whom I also belong,
have to touch the goddess's foot with their own foot, whereupon the image gives them a sign or an oracular utterance like
'Vis ut sis.'"*

343   In this dream the bear-goddess emerges plainly, although her
statue "cannot be seen clearly." The relationship to the self,
the supraordinate personality, is indicated not only by the oracle
"Vis ut sis" but by the quaternity and the circular central
precinct of the temple. From ancient times any relationship to
the stars has always symbolized eternity. The soul comes "from
the stars" and returns to the stellar regions. "Ursanna's" relation to the moon is indicated by the "moon-bowl."

344   The moon-goddess also appears in children's dreams. A girl
who grew up in peculiarly difficult psychic circumstances had
a recurrent dream between her seventh and tenth years: *"The
moon-lady was always waiting for me down by the water at the
landing-stage, to take me to her island."* Unfortunately she
could never remember what happened there, but it was so
beautiful that she often prayed she might have this dream
again. Although, as is evident, the two dreamers are not identical, the *island motif* also occurred in the previous dream as the
inaccessible mountain crest.

345   Thirty years later, the dreamer of the moon-lady had a
dramatic fantasy:

346   *"I am climbing a steep dark mountain, on top of which
stands a domed castle. I enter and go up a winding stairway to
the left. Arriving inside the dome, I find myself in the presence
of a woman wearing a head-dress of cow's horns. I recognize her
immediately as the moon-lady of my childhood dreams. At her
behest I look to the right and see a dazzlingly bright sun shining
on the other side of a deep chasm. Over the chasm stretches a
narrow, transparent bridge, upon which I step, conscious of the
fact that in no circumstances must I look down. An uncanny
fear seizes me, and I hesitate. Treachery seems to be in the air,
but at last I go across and stand before the sun. The sun speaks:
'If you can approach me nine times without being burned, all
will be well.' But I grow more and more afraid, finally I do
look down, and I see a black tentacle like that of an octopus
groping towards me from underneath the sun. I step back in
fright and plunge into the abyss. But instead of being dashed*

to pieces I lie in the arms of the Earth Mother. When I try to look into her face, she turns to clay, and I find myself lying on the earth."

347   It is remarkable how the beginning of this fantasy agrees with the dream. The moon-lady above is clearly distinguished from the Earth Mother below. The former urges the dreamer to her somewhat perilous adventure with the sun; the latter catches her protectively in her maternal arms. The dreamer, as the one in danger, would therefore seem to be in the role of the Kore.

348   Let us now turn back to our dream-series:

349   iii. *Y sees two pictures in a dream, painted by the Scandinavian painter Hermann Christian Lund.*

I. *"The first picture is of a Scandinavian peasant room. Peasant girls in gay costumes are walking about arm in arm (that is, in a row). The middle one is smaller than the rest and, besides this, has a hump and keeps turning her head back. This, together with her peculiar glance, gives her a witchlike look."*

II. *"The second picture shows a dragon with its neck stretched out over the whole picture and especially over a girl, who is in the dragon's power and cannot move, for as soon as she moves, the dragon, which can make its body big or little at will, moves too; and when the girl wants to get away it simply stretches out its neck over her, and so catches her again. Strangely enough, the girl has no face, at least I couldn't see it."*

350   The painter is an invention of the dream. The animus often appears as a painter or has some kind of projection apparatus, or is a cinema-operator or owner of a picture-gallery. All this refers to the animus as the function mediating between conscious and unconscious: the unconscious contains pictures which are transmitted, that is, made manifest, by the animus, either as fantasies or, unconsciously, in the patient's own life and actions. The animus-projection gives rise to fantasied relations of love and hatred for "heroes" or "demons." The favourite victims are tenors, artists, movie-stars, athletic champions, etc. In the first picture the maiden is characterized as demonic, with a hump and an evil look "over her shoulder." (Hence amulets against the evil eye are often worn by primitives on the nape of the neck, for the vulnerable spot is at the back, where you can't see.)

51 In the second picture the "maiden" is portrayed as the inno-cent victim of the monster. Just as before there was a rela-tionship of identity between the sky-woman and the bear, so here between the young girl and the dragon—which in practical life is often rather more than just a bad joke. Here it signifies a widening of the conscious personality, i.e., through the helplessness of the victim on the one hand and the dangers of the humpback's evil eye and the dragon's might on the other.

52 iv (part dream, part visual imagination). *"A magician is demonstrating his tricks to an Indian prince. He produces a beautiful young girl from under a cloth. She is a dancer, who has the power to change her shape or at least hold her audience spell-bound by faultless illusion. During the dance she dissolves with the music into a swarm of bees. Then she changes into a leopard, then into a jet of water, then into an octopus that has twined itself about a young pearl-fisher. Between times, she takes human form again at the dramatic moment. She appears as a she-ass bearing two baskets of wonderful fruits. Then she becomes a many-coloured peacock. The prince is beside him-self with delight and calls her to him. But she dances on, now naked, and even tears the skin from her body, and finally falls down—a naked skeleton. This is buried, but at night a lily grows out of the grave, and from its cup there rises a white lady, who floats slowly up to the sky."*

53 This piece describes the successive transformations of the illusionist (artistry in illusion being a specifically feminine talent) until she becomes a transfigured personality. The fantasy was not invented as a sort of allegory; it was part dream, part spontaneous imagery.

54 v. *"I am in a church made of grey sandstone. The apse is built rather high. Near the tabernacle a girl in a red dress is hanging on the stone cross of the window. (Suicide?)"*

55 Just as in the preceding cases the sacrifice of a child or a sheep played a part, so here the sacrifice of the maiden hanging on the "cross." The death of the dancer is also to be understood in this sense, for these maidens are always doomed to die, be-cause their exclusive domination of the feminine psyche hinders the individuation process, that is, the maturation of personality. The "maiden" corresponds to the anima of the man and makes use of it to gain her natural ends, in which illusion plays the

greatest role imaginable. But as long as a woman is content to be a *femme à homme,* she has no feminine individuality. She is empty and merely glitters—a welcome vessel for masculine projections. Woman as a personality, however, is a very different thing: here illusion no longer works. So that when the question of personality arises, which is as a rule the painful fact of the second half of life, the childish form of the self disappears too.

356   All that remains for me now is to describe the Kore as observable in man, the *anima.* Since a man's wholeness, in so far as he is not constitutionally homosexual, can only be a masculine personality, the feminine figure of the anima cannot be catalogued as a type of supraordinate personality but requires a different evaluation and position. In the products of unconscious activity, the anima appears equally as maiden and mother, which is why a personalistic interpretation always reduces her to the personal mother or some other female person. The real meaning of the figure naturally gets lost in the process, as is inevitably the case with all these reductive interpretations whether in the sphere of the psychology of the unconscious or of mythology. The innumerable attempts that have been made in the sphere of mythology to interpret gods and heroes in a solar, lunar, astral, or meteorological sense contribute nothing of importance to the understanding of them; on the contrary, they all put us on a false track. When, therefore, in dreams and other spontaneous products, we meet with an unknown female figure whose significance oscillates between the extremes of goddess and whore, it is advisable to let her keep her independence and not reduce her arbitrarily to something known. If the unconscious shows her as an "unknown," this attribute should not be got rid of by main force with a view to arriving at a "rational" interpretation. Like the "supraordinate personality," the anima is bipolar and can therefore appear positive one moment and negative the next; now young, now old; now mother, now maiden; now a good fairy, now a witch; now a saint, now a whore. Besides this ambivalence, the anima also has "occult" connections with "mysteries," with the world of darkness in general, and for that reason she often has a religious tinge. Whenever she emerges with some degree of clarity, she always has a peculiar relationship to *time:* as a rule she is more or less immortal, because outside time. Writers who have tried

their hand at this figure have never failed to stress the anima's peculiarity in this respect. I would refer to the classic descriptions in Rider Haggard's *She* and *The Return of She,* in Pierre Benoît's *L'Atlantide,* and above all in the novel of the young American author, William M. Sloane, *To Walk the Night.* In all these accounts, the anima is outside time as we know it and consequently immensely old or a being who belongs to a different order of things.

357   Since we can no longer or only partially express the archetypes of the unconscious by means of figures in which we religiously believe, they lapse into unconsciousness again and hence are unconsciously projected upon more or less suitable human personalities. To the young boy a clearly discernible anima-form appears in his mother, and this lends her the radiance of power and superiority or else a daemonic aura of even greater fascination. But because of the anima's ambivalence, the projection can be entirely negative. Much of the fear which the female sex arouses in men is due to the projection of the anima-image. An infantile man generally has a maternal anima; an adult man, the figure of a younger woman. The senile man finds compensation in a very young girl, or even a child.

[3. Case Z]

358   The anima also has affinities with animals, which symbolize her characteristics. Thus she can appear as a snake or a tiger or a bird. I quote by way of example a dream-series that contains transformations of this kind: [14]

359   i. *A white bird perches on a table. Suddenly it changes into a fair-haired seven-year-old girl and just as suddenly back into a bird, which now speaks with a human voice.*

360   ii. *In an underground house, which is really the underworld, there lives an old magician and prophet with his "daughter." She is, however, not really his daughter; she is a dancer, a very loose person, but is blind and seeks healing.*

361   iii. *A lonely house in a wood, where an old scholar is living. Suddenly his daughter appears, a kind of ghost, complaining that people only look upon her as a figment of fancy.*

[14] Only extracts from the dreams are given, so far as they bear on the anima.

362   iv. *On the façade of a church there is a Gothic Madonna, who is alive and is the "unknown and yet known woman." Instead of a child, she holds in her arms a sort of flame or a snake or a dragon.*

363   v. *A black-clad "countess" kneels in a dark chapel. Her dress is hung with costly pearls. She has red hair, and there is something uncanny about her. Moreover, she is surrounded by the spirits of the dead.*

364   vi. *A female snake comports herself tenderly and insinuatingly, speaking with a human voice. She is only "accidentally" shaped like a snake.*

365   vii. *A bird speaks with the same voice, but shows herself helpful by trying to rescue the dreamer from a dangerous situation.*

366   viii. *The unknown woman sits, like the dreamer, on the tip of a church-spire and stares at him uncannily across the abyss.*

367   ix. *The unknown woman suddenly appears as an old female attendant in an underground public lavatory with a temperature of 40° below zero.*

368   x. *The unknown woman leaves the house as a* petite bourgeoise *with a female relation, and in her place there is suddenly an over-life-size goddess clad in blue, looking like Athene.*

369   xi. *Then she appears in a church, taking the place of the altar, still over-life-size but with veiled face.*

370   In all these dreams [15] the central figure is a mysterious feminine being with qualities like those of no woman known to the dreamer. The unknown is described as such in the dreams themselves, and reveals her extraordinary nature firstly by her power to change shape and secondly by her paradoxical ambivalence. Every conceivable shade of meaning glitters in her, from the highest to the lowest.

371   *Dream i* shows the anima as elflike, i.e., only partially human. She can just as well be a bird, which means that she may belong wholly to nature and can vanish (i.e., become unconscious) from the human sphere (i.e., consciousness).

372   *Dream ii* shows the unknown woman as a mythological figure from the beyond (the unconscious). She is the *soror* or *filia mystica* of a hierophant or "philosopher," evidently a parallel to

[15] The following statements are not meant as "interpretations" of the dreams. They are intended only to sum up the various forms in which the anima appears.

those mystic syzygies which are to be met with in the figures of Simon Magus and Helen, Zosimus and Theosebeia, Comarius and Cleopatra, etc. Our dream-figure fits in best with Helen. A really admirable description of anima-psychology in a woman is to be found in Erskine's *Helen of Troy*.

373   *Dream iii* presents the same theme, but on a more "fairytale-like" plane. Here the anima is shown as rather spookish.

374   *Dream iv* brings the anima nearer to the Mother of God. The "child" refers to the mystic speculations on the subject of the redemptive serpent and the "fiery" nature of the redeemer.

375   In *dream v,* the anima is visualized somewhat romantically as the "distinguished" fascinating woman, who nevertheless has dealings with spirits.

376   *Dreams vi and vii* bring theriomorphic variations. The anima's identity is at once apparent to the dreamer because of the voice and what it says. The anima has "accidentally" taken the form of a snake, just as in *dream i* she changed with the greatest ease into a bird and back again. As a snake, she is playing the negative role, as a bird the positive.

377   *Dream viii* shows the dreamer confronted with his anima. This takes place high above the ground (i.e., above human reality). Obviously it is a case of dangerous fascination by the anima.

378   *Dream ix* signifies the anima's deep plunge into an extremely "subordinate" position, where the last trace of fascination has gone and only human sympathy is left.

379   *Dream x* shows the paradoxical double nature of the anima: banal mediocrity and Olympian divinity.

380   *Dream xi* restores the anima to the Christian church, not as an icon but as the altar itself. The altar is the place of sacrifice and also the receptacle for consecrated relics.

381   To throw even a moderate light on all these anima associations would require special and very extensive investigation, which would be out of place here because, as we have already said, the anima has only an indirect bearing on the interpretation of the Kore figure. I have presented this dream-series simply for the purpose of giving the reader some idea of the empirical material on which the idea of the anima is based.[16] From this series and others like it we get an average picture of that strange factor which has such an important part to play in the

16 Cf. the third paper in this volume.

masculine psyche, and which naïve presumption invariably identifies with certain women, imputing to them all the illusions that swarm in the male Eros.

382   It seems clear enough that the man's anima found occasion for projection in the Demeter cult. The Kore doomed to her subterranean fate, the two-faced mother, and the theriomorphic aspects of both afforded the anima ample opportunity to reflect herself, shimmering and equivocal, in the Eleusinian cult, or rather to experience herself there and fill the celebrants with her unearthly essence, to their lasting gain. For a man, anima experiences are always of immense and abiding significance.

383   But the Demeter-Kore myth is far too feminine to have been merely the result of an anima-projection. Although the anima can, as we have said, experience herself in Demeter-Kore, she is yet of a wholly different nature. She is in the highest degree *femme à homme,* whereas Demeter-Kore exists on the plane of mother-daughter experience, which is alien to man and shuts him out. In fact, the psychology of the Demeter cult bears all the features of a matriarchal order of society, where the man is an indispensable but on the whole disturbing factor.

THE SHADOW AND THE SYZYGY

1: THE SHADOW

13   Whereas the contents of the personal unconscious are acquired during the individual's lifetime, the contents of the collective unconscious are invariably archetypes that were present from the beginning. Their relation to the instincts has been discussed elsewhere.[1] The archetypes most clearly characterized from the empirical point of view are those which have the most frequent and the most disturbing influence on the ego. These are the *shadow,* the *anima,* and the *animus.*[2] The most accessible of these, and the easiest to experience, is the shadow, for its nature can in large measure be inferred from the contents of the personal unconscious. The only exceptions to this rule are those rather rare cases where the positive qualities of the personality are repressed, and the ego in consequence plays an essentially negative or unfavourable role.

14   The shadow is a moral problem that challenges the whole ego-personality, for no one can become conscious of the shadow without considerable moral effort. To become conscious of it involves recognizing the dark aspects of the personality as present and real. This act is the essential condition for any kind of self-knowledge, and it therefore, as a rule, meets with considerable resistance. Indeed, self-knowledge as a psychotherapeutic measure frequently requires much painstaking work extending over a long period.

15   Closer examination of the dark characteristics—that is, the inferiorities constituting the shadow—reveals that they have an *emotional* nature, a kind of autonomy, and accordingly an obsessive or, better, possessive quality. Emotion, incidentally, is

---

1 "Instinct and the Unconscious" and "On the Nature of the Psyche," pars. 397ff.
2 The contents of this and the following chapter are taken from a lecture delivered to the Swiss Society for Practical Psychology, in Zurich, 1948. The material was first published in the *Wiener Zeitschrift für Nervenheilkunde und deren Grenzgebiete,* I (1948) : 4.

not an activity of the individual but something that happens to him. Affects occur usually where adaptation is weakest, and at the same time they reveal the reason for its weakness, namely a certain degree of inferiority and the existence of a lower level of personality. On this lower level with its uncontrolled or scarcely controlled emotions one behaves more or less like a primitive, who is not only the passive victim of his affects but also singularly incapable of moral judgment.

16 Although, with insight and good will, the shadow can to some extent be assimilated into the conscious personality, experience shows that there are certain features which offer the most obstinate resistance to moral control and prove almost impossible to influence. These resistances are usually bound up with *projections,* which are not recognized as such, and their recognition is a moral achievement beyond the ordinary. While some traits peculiar to the shadow can be recognized without too much difficulty as one's own personal qualities, in this case both insight and good will are unavailing because the cause of the emotion appears to lie, beyond all possibility of doubt, in the *other person.* No matter how obvious it may be to the neutral observer that it is a matter of projections, there is little hope that the subject will perceive this himself. He must be convinced that he throws a very long shadow before he is willing to withdraw his emotionally-toned projections from their object.

17 Let us suppose that a certain individual shows no inclination whatever to recognize his projections. The projection-making factor then has a free hand and can realize its object—if it has one—or bring about some other situation characteristic of its power. As we know, it is not the conscious subject but the unconscious which does the projecting. Hence one meets with projections, one does not make them. The effect of projection is to isolate the subject from his environment, since instead of a real relation to it there is now only an illusory one. Projections change the world into the replica of one's own unknown face. In the last analysis, therefore, they lead to an autoerotic or autistic condition in which one dreams a world whose reality remains forever unattainable. The resultant *sentiment d'incomplétude* and the still worse feeling of sterility are in their turn explained by projection as the malevolence of the environment, and by means of this vicious circle the isolation is intensified. The more

projections are thrust in between the subject and the environment, the harder it is for the ego to see through its illusions. A
forty-five-year-old patient who had suffered from a compulsion
neurosis since he was twenty and had become completely cut off
from the world once said to me: "But I can never admit to myself that I've wasted the best twenty-five years of my life!"

18   It is often tragic to see how blatantly a man bungles his own
life and the lives of others yet remains totally incapable of seeing how much the whole tragedy originates in himself, and how
he continually feeds it and keeps it going. Not *consciously,* of
course—for consciously he is engaged in bewailing and cursing a
faithless world that recedes further and further into the distance. Rather, it is an unconscious factor which spins the illusions that veil his world. And what is being spun is a cocoon,
which in the end will completely envelop him.

19   One might assume that projections like these, which are so
very difficult if not impossible to dissolve, would belong to the
realm of the shadow—that is, to the negative side of the personality. This assumption becomes untenable after a certain point,
because the symbols that then appear no longer refer to the
same but to the opposite sex, in a man's case to a woman and
vice versa. The source of projections is no longer the shadow—
which is always of the same sex as the subject—but a contrasexual
figure. Here we meet the animus of a woman and the anima of a
man, two corresponding archetypes whose autonomy and unconsciousness explain the stubbornness of their projections. Though
the shadow is a motif as well known to mythology as anima and
animus, it represents first and foremost the personal unconscious, and its content can therefore be made conscious without
too much difficulty. In this it differs from anima and animus,
for whereas the shadow can be seen through and recognized
fairly easily, the anima and animus are much further away from
consciousness and in normal circumstances are seldom if ever
realized. With a little self-criticism one can see through the
shadow—so far as its nature is personal. But when it appears as
an archetype, one encounters the same difficulties as with anima
and animus. In other words, it is quite within the bounds of
possibility for a man to recognize the relative evil of his nature,
but it is a rare and shattering experience for him to gaze into
the face of absolute evil.

20   What, then, is this projection-making factor? The East calls
it the "Spinning Woman" [1]—Maya, who creates illusion by her
dancing. Had we not long since known it from the symbolism
of dreams, this hint from the Orient would put us on the right
track: the enveloping, embracing, and devouring element points
unmistakably to the mother,[2] that is, to the son's relation to the
real mother, to her imago, and to the woman who is to become
a mother for him. His Eros is passive like a child's; he hopes to
be caught, sucked in, enveloped, and devoured. He seeks, as it
were, the protecting, nourishing, charmed circle of the mother,
the condition of the infant released from every care, in which
the outside world bends over him and even forces happiness
upon him. No wonder the real world vanishes from sight!

21   If this situation is dramatized, as the unconscious usually
dramatizes it, then there appears before you on the psychological
stage a man living regressively, seeking his childhood and his
mother, fleeing from a cold cruel world which denies him understanding. Often a mother appears beside him who apparently
shows not the slightest concern that her little son should become
a man, but who, with tireless and self-immolating effort, neglects
nothing that might hinder him from growing up and marrying.
You behold the secret conspiracy between mother and son, and
how each helps the other to betray life.

22   Where does the guilt lie? With the mother, or with the son?
Probably with both. The unsatisfied longing of the son for life
and the world ought to be taken seriously. There is in him a

1 Erwin Rousselle, "Seelische Führung im lebenden Taoismus," Pl. I, pp. 150, 170.
Rousselle calls the spinning woman the "animal soul." There is a saying that
runs, "The spinner sets in motion." I have defined the anima as a personification
of the unconscious.
2 Here and in what follows, the word "mother" is not meant in the literal sense
but as a symbol of everything that functions as a mother.

desire to touch reality, to embrace the earth and fructify the field of the world. But he makes no more than a series of fitful starts, for his initiative as well as his staying power are crippled by the secret memory that the world and happiness may be had as a gift—from the mother. The fragment of world which he, like every man, must encounter again and again is never quite the right one, since it does not fall into his lap, does not meet him half way, but remains resistant, has to be conquered, and submits only to force. It makes demands on the masculinity of a man, on his ardour, above all on his courage and resolution when it comes to throwing his whole being into the scales. For this he would need a faithless Eros, one capable of forgetting his mother and undergoing the pain of relinquishing the first love of his life. The mother, foreseeing this danger, has carefully inculcated into him the virtues of faithfulness, devotion, loyalty, so as to protect him from the moral disruption which is the risk of every life adventure. He has learnt these lessons only too well, and remains true to his mother. This naturally causes her the deepest anxiety (when, to her greater glory, he turns out to be a homosexual, for example) and at the same time affords her an unconscious satisfaction that is positively mythological. For, in the relationship now reigning between them, there is consummated the immemorial and most sacred archetype of the marriage of mother and son. What, after all, has commonplace reality to offer, with its registry offices, pay envelopes, and monthly rent, that could outweigh the mystic awe of the *hieros gamos*? Or the star-crowned woman whom the dragon pursues, or the pious obscurities veiling the marriage of the Lamb?

23   This myth, better than any other, illustrates the nature of the collective unconscious. At this level the mother is both old and young, Demeter and Persephone, and the son is spouse and sleeping suckling rolled into one. The imperfections of real life, with its laborious adaptations and manifold disappointments, naturally cannot compete with such a state of indescribable fulfilment.

24   In the case of the son, the projection-making factor is identical with the mother-imago, and this is consequently taken to be the real mother. The projection can only be dissolved when the son sees that in the realm of his psyche there is an imago not only of the mother but of the daughter, the sister, the beloved,

the heavenly goddess, and the chthonic Baubo. Every mother and every beloved is forced to become the carrier and embodiment of this omnipresent and ageless image, which corresponds to the deepest reality in a man. It belongs to him, this perilous image of Woman; she stands for the loyalty which in the interests of life he must sometimes forgo; she is the much needed compensation for the risks, struggles, sacrifices that all end in disappointment; she is the solace for all the bitterness of life. And, at the same time, she is the great illusionist, the seductress, who draws him into life with her Maya—and not only into life's reasonable and useful aspects, but into its frightful paradoxes and ambivalences where good and evil, success and ruin, hope and despair, counterbalance one another. Because she is his greatest danger she demands from a man his greatest, and if he has it in him she will receive it.

25   This image is "My Lady Soul," as Spitteler called her. I have suggested instead the term "anima," as indicating something specific, for which the expression "soul" is too general and too vague. The empirical reality summed up under the concept of the anima forms an extremely dramatic content of the unconscious. It is possible to describe this content in rational, scientific language, but in this way one entirely fails to express its living character. Therefore, in describing the living processes of the psyche, I deliberately and consciously give preference to a dramatic, mythological way of thinking and speaking, because this is not only more expressive but also more exact than an abstract scientific terminology, which is wont to toy with the notion that its theoretic formulations may one fine day be resolved into algebraic equations.

26   The projection-making factor is the anima, or rather the unconscious as represented by the anima. Whenever she appears, in dreams, visions, and fantasies, she takes on personified form, thus demonstrating that the factor she embodies possesses all the outstanding characteristics of a feminine being.[3] She is not an invention of the conscious, but a spontaneous product of the

---

[3] Naturally, she is a typical figure in *belles-lettres*. Recent publications on the subject of the anima include Linda Fierz-David, *The Dream of Poliphilo*, and my "Psychology of the Transference." The anima as a psychological idea first appears in the 16th-cent. humanist Richardus Vitus. Cf. my *Mysterium Coniunctionis*, pars. 91ff.

unconscious. Nor is she a substitute figure for the mother. On the contrary, there is every likelihood that the numinous qualities which make the mother-imago so dangerously powerful derive from the collective archetype of the anima, which is incarnated anew in every male child.

27   Since the anima is an archetype that is found in men, it is reasonable to suppose that an equivalent archetype must be present in women; for just as the man is compensated by a feminine element, so woman is compensated by a masculine one. I do not, however, wish this argument to give the impression that these compensatory relationships were arrived at by deduction. On the contrary, long and varied experience was needed in order to grasp the nature of anima and animus empirically. Whatever we have to say about these archetypes, therefore, is either directly verifiable or at least rendered probable by the facts. At the same time, I am fully aware that we are discussing pioneer work which by its very nature can only be provisional.

28   Just as the mother seems to be the first carrier of the projection-making factor for the son, so is the father for the daughter. Practical experience of these relationships is made up of many individual cases presenting all kinds of variations on the same basic theme. A concise description of them can, therefore, be no more than schematic.

29   Woman is compensated by a masculine element and therefore her unconscious has, so to speak, a masculine imprint. This results in a considerable psychological difference between men and women, and accordingly I have called the projection-making factor in women the animus, which means mind or spirit. The animus corresponds to the paternal Logos just as the anima corresponds to the maternal Eros. But I do not wish or intend to give these two intuitive concepts too specific a definition. I use Eros and Logos merely as conceptual aids to describe the fact that woman's consciousness is characterized more by the connective quality of Eros than by the discrimination and cognition associated with Logos. In men, Eros, the function of relationship, is usually less developed than Logos. In women, on the other hand, Eros is an expression of their true nature, while their Logos is often only a regrettable accident. It gives rise to misunderstandings and annoying interpretations in the family

circle and among friends. This is because it consists of *opinions* instead of reflections, and by opinions I mean *a priori* assumptions that lay claim to absolute truth. Such assumptions, as everyone knows, can be extremely irritating. As the animus is partial to argument, he can best be seen at work in disputes where both parties know they are right. Men can argue in a very womanish way, too, when they are anima-possessed and have thus been transformed into the animus of their own anima. With them the question becomes one of personal vanity and touchiness (as if they were females); with women it is a question of *power*, whether of truth or justice or some other "ism"—for the dressmaker and hairdresser have already taken care of their vanity. The "Father" (i.e., the sum of conventional opinions) always plays a great role in female argumentation. No matter how friendly and obliging a woman's Eros may be, no logic on earth can shake her if she is ridden by the animus. Often the man has the feeling—and he is not altogether wrong—that only seduction or a beating or rape would have the necessary power of persuasion. He is unaware that this highly dramatic situation would instantly come to a banal and unexciting end if he were to quit the field and let a second woman carry on the battle (his wife, for instance, if she herself is not the fiery war horse). This sound idea seldom or never occurs to him, because no man can converse with an animus for five minutes without becoming the victim of his own anima. Anyone who still had enough sense of humour to listen objectively to the ensuing dialogue would be staggered by the vast number of commonplaces, misapplied truisms, clichés from newspapers and novels, shopsoiled platitudes of every description interspersed with vulgar abuse and brain-splitting lack of logic. It is a dialogue which, irrespective of its participants, is repeated millions and millions of times in all the languages of the world and always remains essentially the same.

30   This singular fact is due to the following circumstance: when animus and anima meet, the animus draws his sword of power and the anima ejects her poison of illusion and seduction. The outcome need not always be negative, since the two are equally likely to fall in love (a special instance of love at first sight). The language of love is of astonishing uniformity, using the well-worn formulas with the utmost devotion and fidelity,

so that once again the two partners find themselves in a banal collective situation. Yet they live in the illusion that they are related to one another in a most individual way.

31   In both its positive and its negative aspects the anima/animus relationship is always full of "animosity," i.e., it is emotional, and hence collective. Affects lower the level of the relationship and bring it closer to the common instinctual basis, which no longer has anything individual about it. Very often the relationship runs its course heedless of its human performers, who afterwards do not know what happened to them.

32   Whereas the cloud of "animosity" surrounding the man is composed chiefly of sentimentality and resentment, in woman it expresses itself in the form of opinionated views, interpretations, insinuations, and misconstructions, which all have the purpose (sometimes attained) of severing the relation between two human beings. The woman, like the man, becomes wrapped in a veil of illusions by her demon-familiar, and, as the daughter who alone understands her father (that is, is eternally right in everything), she is translated to the land of sheep, where she is put to graze by the shepherd of her soul, the animus.

33   Like the anima, the animus too has a positive aspect. Through the figure of the father he expresses not only conventional opinion but—equally—what we call "spirit," philosophical or religious ideas in particular, or rather the attitude resulting from them. Thus the animus is a psychopomp, a mediator between the conscious and the unconscious and a personification of the latter. Just as the anima becomes, through integration, the Eros of consciousness, so the animus becomes a Logos; and in the same way that the anima gives relationship and relatedness to a man's consciousness, the animus gives to woman's consciousness a capacity for reflection, deliberation, and self-knowledge.

34   The effect of anima and animus on the ego is in principle the same. This effect is extremely difficult to eliminate because, in the first place, it is uncommonly strong and immediately fills the ego-personality with an unshakable feeling of rightness and righteousness. In the second place, the cause of the effect is projected and appears to lie in objects and objective situations. Both these characteristics can, I believe, be traced back to the peculiarities of the archetype. For the archetype, of course, exists

a priori. This may possibly explain the often totally irrational yet undisputed and indisputable existence of certain moods and opinions. Perhaps these are so notoriously difficult to influence because of the powerfully suggestive effect emanating from the archetype. Consciousness is fascinated by it, held captive, as if hypnotized. Very often the ego experiences a vague feeling of moral defeat and then behaves all the more defensively, defiantly, and self-righteously, thus setting up a vicious circle which only increases its feeling of inferiority. The bottom is then knocked out of the human relationship, for, like megalomania, a feeling of inferiority makes mutual recognition impossible, and without this there is no relationship.

35   As I said, it is easier to gain insight into the shadow than into the anima or animus. With the shadow, we have the advantage of being prepared in some sort by our education, which has always endeavoured to convince people that they are not one-hundred-per-cent pure gold. So everyone immediately understands what is meant by "shadow," "inferior personality," etc. And if he has forgotten, his memory can easily be refreshed by a Sunday sermon, his wife, or the tax collector. With the anima and animus, however, things are by no means so simple. Firstly, there is no moral education in this respect, and secondly, most people are content to be self-righteous and prefer mutual vilification (if nothing worse!) to the recognition of their projections. Indeed, it seems a very natural state of affairs for men to have irrational moods and women irrational opinions. Presumably this situation is grounded on instinct and must remain as it is to ensure that the Empedoclean game of the hate and love of the elements shall continue for all eternity. Nature is conservative and does not easily allow her courses to be altered; she defends in the most stubborn way the inviolability of the preserves where anima and animus roam, Hence it is much more difficult to become conscious of one's anima/animus projections than to acknowledge one's shadow side. One has, of course, to overcome certain moral obstacles, such as vanity, ambition, conceit, resentment, etc., but in the case of projections all sorts of purely intellectual difficulties are added, quite apart from the contents of the projection which one simply doesn't know how to cope with. And on top of all this there arises a profound doubt as to whether one is not meddling too much with nature's

business by prodding into consciousness things which it would have been better to leave asleep.

36   Although there are, in my experience, a fair number of people who can understand without special intellectual or moral difficulties what is meant by anima and animus, one finds very many more who have the greatest trouble in visualizing these empirical concepts as anything concrete. This shows that they fall a little outside the usual range of experience. They are unpopular precisely because they seem unfamiliar. The consequence is that they mobilize prejudice and become taboo like everything else that is unexpected.

37   So if we set it up as a kind of requirement that projections should be dissolved, because it is wholesomer that way and in every respect more advantageous, we are entering upon new ground. Up till now everybody has been convinced that the idea "my father," "my mother," etc., is nothing but a faithful reflection of the real parent, corresponding in every detail to the original, so that when someone says "my father" he means no more and no less than what his father is in reality. This is actually what he supposes he does mean, but a supposition of identity by no means brings that identity about. This is where the fallacy of the *enkekalymmenos* ('the veiled one') comes in.[4] If one includes in the psychological equation X's picture of his father, which he takes for the real father, the equation will not work out, because the unknown quantity he has introduced does not tally with reality. X has overlooked the fact that his idea of a person consists, in the first place, of the possibly very incomplete picture he has received of the real person and, in the second place, of the subjective modifications he has imposed upon this picture. X's idea of his father is a complex quantity for which the real father is only in part responsible, an indefinitely larger share falling to the son. So true is this that every time he criticizes or praises his father he is unconsciously hitting back at himself, thereby bringing about those psychic consequences that overtake people who habitually disparage or overpraise themselves. If, however, X carefully compares his reactions with reality, he stands a chance of noticing that he has miscalculated

4 The fallacy, which stems from Eubulides the Megarian, runs: "Can you recognize your father?" Yes. "Can you recognize this veiled one?" No. "This veiled one is your father. Hence you can recognize your father and not recognize him."

somewhere by not realizing long ago from his father's behaviour that the picture he has of him is a false one. But as a rule X is convinced that he is right, and if anybody is wrong it must be the other fellow. Should X have a poorly developed Eros, he will be either indifferent to the inadequate relationship he has with his father or else annoyed by the inconsistency and general incomprehensibility of a father whose behaviour never really corresponds to the picture X has of him. Therefore X thinks he has every right to feel hurt, misunderstood, and even betrayed.

38   One can imagine how desirable it would be in such cases to dissolve the projection. And there are always optimists who believe that the golden age can be ushered in simply by telling people the right way to go. But just let them try to explain to these people that they are acting like a dog chasing its own tail. To make a person see the shortcomings of his attitude considerably more than mere "telling" is needed, for more is involved than ordinary common sense can allow. What one is up against here is the kind of fateful misunderstanding which, under ordinary conditions, remains forever inaccessible to insight. It is rather like expecting the average respectable citizen to recognize himself as a criminal.

39   I mention all this just to illustrate the order of magnitude to which the anima/animus projections belong, and the moral and intellectual exertions that are needed to dissolve them. Not all the contents of the anima and animus are projected, however. Many of them appear spontaneously in dreams and so on, and many more can be made conscious through active imagination. In this way we find that thoughts, feelings, and affects are alive in us which we would never have believed possible. Naturally, possibilities of this sort seem utterly fantastic to anyone who has not experienced them himself, for a normal person "knows what he thinks." Such a childish attitude on the part of the "normal person" is simply the rule, so that no one without experience in this field can be expected to understand the real nature of anima and animus. With these reflections one gets into an entirely new world of psychological experience, provided of course that one succeeds in realizing it in practice. Those who do succeed can hardly fail to be impressed by all that the ego does not know and never has known. This increase in self-knowledge is still very rare nowadays and is usually

paid for in advance with a neurosis, if not with something worse.

40   The autonomy of the collective unconscious expresses itself in the figures of anima and animus. They personify those of its contents which, when withdrawn from projection, can be integrated into consciousness. To this extent, both figures represent *functions* which filter the contents of the collective unconscious through to the conscious mind. They appear or behave as such, however, only so long as the tendencies of the conscious and unconscious do not diverge too greatly. Should any tension arise, these functions, harmless till then, confront the conscious mind in personified form and behave rather like systems split off from the personality, or like part souls. This comparison is inadequate in so far as nothing previously belonging to the ego-personality has split off from it; on the contrary, the two figures represent a disturbing accretion. The reason for their behaving in this way is that though the *contents* of anima and animus can be integrated they themselves cannot, since they are archetypes. As such they are the foundation stones of the psychic structure, which in its totality exceeds the limits of consciousness and therefore can never become the object of direct cognition. Though the effects of anima and animus can be made conscious, they themselves are factors transcending consciousness and beyond the reach of perception and volition. Hence they remain autonomous despite the integration of their contents, and for this reason they should be borne constantly in mind. This is extremely important from the therapeutic standpoint, because constant observation pays the unconscious a tribute that more or less guarantees its co-operation. The unconscious as we know can never be "done with" once and for all. It is, in fact, one of the most important tasks of psychic hygiene to pay continual attention to the symptomatology of unconscious contents and processes, for the good reason that the conscious mind is always in danger of becoming one-sided, of keeping to well-worn paths and getting stuck in blind alleys. The complementary and compensating function of the unconscious ensures that these dangers, which are especially great in neurosis, can in some measure be avoided. It is only under ideal conditions, when life is still simple and unconscious enough to follow the serpentine path of instinct without hesitation or misgiving, that the compensation works with entire success. The more civilized, the more con-

scious and complicated a man is, the less he is able to follow his instincts. His complicated living conditions and the influence of his environment are so strong that they drown the quiet voice of nature. Opinions, beliefs, theories, and collective tendencies appear in its stead and back up all the aberrations of the conscious mind. Deliberate attention should then be given to the unconscious so that the compensation can set to work. Hence it is especially important to picture the archetypes of the unconscious not as a rushing phantasmagoria of fugitive images but as constant, autonomous factors, which indeed they are.

41   Both these archetypes, as practical experience shows, possess a fatality that can on occasion produce tragic results. They are quite literally the father and mother of all the disastrous entanglements of fate and have long been recognized as such by the whole world. Together they form a divine pair,[5] one of whom, in accordance with his Logos nature, is characterized by *pneuma* and *nous*, rather like Hermes with his ever-shifting hues, while the other, in accordance with her Eros nature, wears the features of Aphrodite, Helen (Selene), Persephone, and Hecate. Both of them are unconscious powers, "gods" in fact, as the ancient world quite rightly conceived them to be. To call them by this name is to give them that central position in the scale of psychological values which has always been theirs whether consciously acknowledged or not; for their power grows in proportion to the degree that they remain unconscious. Those who do not see them are in their hands, just as a typhus epidemic flourishes best when its source is undiscovered. Even in Christianity the divine syzygy has not become obsolete, but occupies the highest place as Christ and his bride the Church.[6] Parallels like these prove extremely helpful in our attempts to find the right

[5] Naturally this is not meant as a psychological definition, let alone a metaphysical one. As I pointed out in "The Relations between the Ego and the Unconscious" (pars. 296ff.), the syzygy consists of three elements: the femininity pertaining to the man and the masculinity pertaining to the woman; the experience which man has of woman and vice versa; and, finally, the masculine and feminine archetypal image. The first element can be integrated into the personality by the process of conscious realization, but the last one cannot.

[6] "For the Scripture says, God made man male and female; the male is Christ, the female is the Church."—Second Epistle of Clement to the Corinthians, xiv, 2 (trans. by Lake, I, p. 151). In pictorial representations, Mary often takes the place of the Church.

criterion for gauging the significance of these two archetypes. What we can discover about them from the conscious side is so slight as to be almost imperceptible. It is only when we throw light into the dark depths of the psyche and explore the strange and tortuous paths of human fate that it gradually becomes clear to us how immense is the influence wielded by these two factors that complement our conscious life.

42   Recapitulating, I should like to emphasize that the integration of the shadow, or the realization of the personal unconscious, marks the first stage in the analytic process, and that without it a recognition of anima and animus is impossible. The shadow can be realized only through a relation to a partner, and anima and animus only through a relation to a partner of the opposite sex, because only in such a relation do their projections become operative. The recognition of the anima gives rise, in a man, to a triad, one third of which is transcendent: the masculine subject, the opposing feminine subject, and the transcendent anima. With a woman the situation is reversed. The missing fourth element that would make the triad a quaternity is, in a man, the archetype of the Wise Old Man, which I have not discussed here, and in a woman the Chthonic Mother. These four constitute a half immanent and half transcendent quaternity, an archetype which I have called the *marriage quaternio*.[7] The marriage quaternio provides a schema not only for the self but also for the structure of primitive society with its cross-cousin marriage, marriage classes, and division of settlements into quarters. The self, on the other hand, is a God-image, or at least cannot be distinguished from one. Of this the early Christian spirit was not ignorant, otherwise Clement of Alexandria could never have said that he who knows himself knows God.[8]

---

[7] "The Psychology of the Transference," pars. 425ff. Cf. infra, pars. 358ff., the Naassene *quaternio*.
[8] Cf. infra, par. 347.

THE COLLECTED WORKS OF
C. G. JUNG

THE PUBLICATION of the first complete edition, in English, of the works of C. G. Jung was undertaken by Routledge and Kegan Paul, Ltd., in England and by Bollingen Foundation in the United States. The American edition is number XX in Bollingen Series, which since 1967 has been published by Princeton University Press. The edition contains revised versions of works previously published, such as *Psychology of the Unconscious*, which is now entitled *Symbols of Transformation*; works originally written in English, such as *Psychology and Religion*; works not previously translated, such as *Aion*; and, in general, new translations of virtually all of Professor Jung's writings. Prior to his death, in 1961, the author supervised the textual revision, which in some cases is extensive. Sir Herbert Read (d. 1968), Dr. Michael Fordham, and Dr. Gerhard Adler compose the Editorial Committee; the translator is R. F. C. Hull (except for Volume 2) and William McGuire is executive editor.

The price of the volumes varies according to size; they are sold separately, and may also be obtained on standing order. Several of the volumes are extensively illustrated. Each volume contains an index and in most a bibliography; the final volume will contain a complete bibliography of Professor Jung's writings and a general index to the entire edition.

In the following list, dates of original publication are given in parentheses (of original composition, in brackets). Multiple dates indicate revisions.

* Published 1957; 2nd edn., 1970.   † Published 1973.

Published 1960.   † Published 1961.
Published 1956; 2nd edn., 1967. (65 plates, 43 text figures.)

* Published 1971.   † Published 1953; 2nd edn., 1966.
‡ Published 1960; 2nd edn., 1969.

Psychological Factors Determining Human Behavior (1937)
Instinct and the Unconscious (1919)
The Structure of the Psyche (1927/1931)
On the Nature of the Psyche (1947/1954)
General Aspects of Dream Psychology (1916/1948)
On the Nature of Dreams (1945/1948)
The Psychological Foundations of Belief in Spirits (1920/1948)
Spirit and Life (1926)
Basic Postulates of Analytical Psychology (1931)
Analytical Psychology and *Weltanschauung* (1928/1931)
The Real and the Surreal (1933)
The Stages of Life (1930–1931)
The Soul and Death (1934)
Synchronicity: An Acausal Connecting Principle (1952)
Appendix: On Synchronicity (1951)

*9. PART I. THE ARCHETYPES AND THE
COLLECTIVE UNCONSCIOUS
Archetypes of the Collective Unconscious (1934/1954)
The Concept of the Collective Unconscious (1936)
Concerning the Archetypes, with Special Reference to the Anima
    Concept (1936/1954)
Psychological Aspects of the Mother Archetype (1938/1954)
Concerning Rebirth (1940/1950)
The Psychology of the Child Archetype (1940)
The Psychological Aspects of the Kore (1941)
The Phenomenology of the Spirit in Fairytales (1945/1948)
On the Psychology of the Trickster-Figure (1954)
Conscious, Unconscious, and Individuation (1939)
A Study in the Process of Individuation (1934/1950)
Concerning Mandala Symbolism (1950)
Appendix: Mandalas (1955)

*9. PART II. AION (1951)
    RESEARCHES INTO THE PHENOMENOLOGY OF THE SELF
The Ego
The Shadow
The Syzygy: Anima and Animus
The Self
Christ, a Symbol of the Self
The Sign of the Fishes   (*continued*)

Published 1959; 2nd edn., 1968. (Part I: 79 plates, with 29 in colour.)

* Published 1964; 2nd edn., 1970. (8 plates.)
† Published 1958; 2nd edn., 1969.

A Psychological Approach to the Dogma of the Trinity (1942/1948)
Transformation Symbolism in the Mass (1942/1954)
Forewords to White's "God and the Unconscious" and Werblowsky's
    "Lucifer and Prometheus" (1952)
Brother Klaus (1933)
Psychotherapists or the Clergy (1932)
Psychoanalysis and the Cure of Souls (1928)
Answer to Job (1952)
    EASTERN RELIGION
Psychological Commentaries on "The Tibetan Book of the Great
    Liberation" (1939/1954) and "The Tibetan Book of the Dead"
    (1935/1953)
Yoga and the West (1936)
Foreword to Suzuki's "Introduction to Zen Buddhism" (1939)
The Psychology of Eastern Meditation (1943)
The Holy Men of India: Introduction to Zimmer's "Der Weg zum
    Selbst" (1944)
Foreword to the "I Ching" (1950)

12. PSYCHOLOGY AND ALCHEMY (1944)
    Prefatory note to the English Edition ([1951?] added 1967)
    Introduction to the Religious and Psychological Problems of Alchemy
    Individual Dream Symbolism in Relation to Alchemy (1936)
    Religious Ideas in Alchemy (1937)
    Epilogue

13. ALCHEMICAL STUDIES
    Commentary on "The Secret of the Golden Flower" (1929)
    The Visions of Zosimos (1938/1954)
    Paracelsus as a Spiritual Phenomenon (1942)
    The Spirit Mercurius (1943/1948)
    The Philosophical Tree (1945/1954)

14. MYSTERIUM CONIUNCTIONIS (1955-56)
    AN INQUIRY INTO THE SEPARATION AND
    SYNTHESIS OF PSYCHIC OPPOSITES IN ALCHEMY
    The Components of the Coniunctio
    The Paradoxa
    The Personification of the Opposites
    Rex and Regina   (continued)

Published 1953; 2nd edn., completely revised, 1968. (270 illustrations.)
Published 1968. (50 plates, 4 text figures.)
Published 1963; 2nd edn., 1970. (10 plates.)

* Published 1966.
† Published 1954; 2nd edn., revised and augmented, 1966. (13 illustrations.)
‡ Published 1954.

The Development of Personality (1934)
Marriage as a Psychological Relationship (1925)

*18. THE SYMBOLIC LIFE
Miscellaneous Writings

†19. GENERAL BIBLIOGRAPHY OF C. G. JUNG'S WRITINGS

†20. GENERAL INDEX TO THE COLLECTED WORKS

See also:

C. G. JUNG: LETTERS
Selected and edited by Gerhard Adler, in collaboration with Aniela Jaffé.
Translations from the German by R.F.C. Hull.

VOL. 1: 1906–1950
VOL. 2: 1951–1961

THE FREUD/JUNG LETTERS
Edited by William McGuire, translated by
Ralph Manheim and R.F.C. Hull

C. G. JUNG SPEAKING: Interviews and Encounters
Edited by William McGuire and R.F.C. Hull

* Published 1976.
† Published 1979.

DATE DUE